Beer

and the

Nobel Prize

Curious Tales of the Nobel Prizes and the People Who Won Them

Thomas M. Annesley

Beer and the Nobel Prize
Curious Tales of the Nobel Prizes and the People Who Won Them

Copyright © 2025 by Thomas M. Annesley

ISBN
979-8-9991980-0-6 (paperback)
979-8-9991980-1-3 (epub)

Library of Congress Control Number: 2025912204

Contents

Preface

In 1967, CBS television war correspondent Charles Kuralt proposed to his bosses that they try something new. Kuralt would travel around the USA, uncovering interesting stories. Although his new idea ran into a lukewarm reception, CBS relented and authorized a pilot episode. When *CBS Evening News with Walter Cronkite* aired the first *On the Road* segment, the telephone switchboard lights went crazy. Viewers loved it. A television network was finally presenting untold stories about fellow Americans. Message received. So, for the next quarter-century Kuralt began meandering around the countryside in a travel home, looking for stories that begged to be told. I wanted to be like Charles Kuralt, finding and telling a story.

After Kuralt traded in his last travel home, Steve Hartman took up the mantle of finding captivating stories, even in the smallest of places. Hartman started in 1998 with his biweekly *Everybody Has a Story* series, in which he would throw a dart at a map of the United States and then show America how a random person from the town hit by the dart had a unique story worth telling. Hartman's stories continue to this day with his weekly *On the Road* episodes, where he brings to life stories about unique people with whom he crosses paths. I make sure I am home on Friday at 6:55 p.m. to catch the latest treat from my current storytelling hero.

How did I go from wanting to tell stories just like Charles Kuralt or Steve Hartman to writing a book about curious tales of the Nobel Prizes? Over the years I have been privileged to spend time with numerous Nobel laureates. They have left indelible impressions on me, the vast majority positive. As I sat with them one-on-one or had conversations over dinner, I learned exactly what Steve Hartman meant in a 2010 piece that he wrote for the *CBS Evening News*: "I never dreamed you could actually find good stories like that. Turns out I couldn't have been more wrong. I now believe the white pages are chock full of amazing, untold stories."

These remarkable scientists, economists, writers, theologians, and peacekeepers that I spent time with were also chock full of amazing, untold stories. But how to tell the stories? How tell people something new? What angle to take? That's where a bottle of beer and my own *On the Road* experience came to the rescue.

I had picked up a scientist at the Minneapolis Airport so we could make our short drive to the Nobel Conference in St. Peter, Minnesota. As we drove into town, he noticed a convenience store and asked that I stop so he could pick up a six-pack of beer. It turned out that he was a beer drinker who enjoyed trying out local brews when he traveled. I told him I had a better idea. So, on a Tuesday night, in a small college town roughly sixty miles south of the Twin Cities, this certain Nobel Prize candidate and I sat near the fireplace in the campus guest house, clinking our Grain Belt beer bottles. By my recollection (remember, beer was involved), the conversation went something like this:

> "Wasn't this a better idea?" I asked.
> "Absolutely. This is what life is all about. Cheers."
> "Did you know that the secret to purifying insulin was discovered by an employee at a brewery?"
> "Did you know that the Nobel Committee couldn't reach Peter Higgs to notify him about his winning the Nobel Prize? He was at lunch having a beer. Somebody on the street told him."
> "No, but I know that Carlsberg Brewery gave Niels Bohr free beer for life after he won the Nobel Prize," I said.
> "Everyone knows that."
> "You and I know it, but not everyone."
> "Then somebody needs to tell them."
> "Someone needs to tell people about beer and the Nobel Prize?"
> "An admirable goal if you ask me."
> "Would it be worthy of a Nobel Prize?" I wondered.
> "Who knows. It's worthy of another beer."

This conversation was memorable not because it was about the Nobel Prize, but because it was about beer and the Nobel Prize. Niels Bohr receiving the Nobel Prize might be interesting, but Niels Bohr purportedly being rewarded with free beer for life by proud Danes was just as interesting. The fact that Peter Higgs won a Nobel Prize was interesting. That Peter Higgs had slipped out midday for a beer, missed the call from the Nobel Foundation, and was finally told by someone who recognized him on the street, was equally interesting. And that was just beer and the Nobel Prizes. Just think what other curious tales existed about the Nobel Prizes and the people who had won them.

I would do what my heroes Charles Kuralt and Steve Hartman did so well. I would help people see what lies beyond the typical news reports every October covering the Nobel Prizes. Curious things like losing a newly awarded Nobel gold medal at a bar. Or giving oneself an ulcer to try to heal it later. Or using a fly in a urinal as proof of an economic theory. The "you can't make this stuff up" tales.

As for my famous scientist friend, when he makes his deserved trip to Stockholm, he is going to be disappointed. They serve wine at the Nobel Prize banquet.

CHAPTER ONE

Nobel Prize Word Association

When I was in college, I had a wonderful psychology professor who played a word game with each group of Psychology 101 students. He would ask each student to toss out a noun. Any noun. One student said *cow*. Another said *desk*. Another *baseball*. I even remember *spaghetti* being thrown out. This went on for another dozen or so students. Professor K then used all these nouns to create a story. Professor K amazed us, but since this was a psychology class, he managed to teach us the mental trick to creating a story from a random set of nouns.

I never had the opportunity to take another class from Professor K. I would have loved to up the ante by challenging him to do the opposite, beginning with the story and finding a common element that tied the parts of the story together. My old professor is long gone now, so the challenge now falls on me. Could I start with a real story and find a common association that somehow tied together all the nouns? What if this common element was *Nobel*? And what if every noun had a Nobel story behind it? Well, here goes, using a recent evening at my house:

> *I got up from the **chair** in my den, put away a book on **seashells** I had been reading, and went to the kitchen to pour a glass of cold **water** from a pitcher in the **refrigerator**. Inside the refrigerator door was a container of **yogurt** that I was tempted to grab but decided not to have a late-night snack. I transferred my pocket change to the **coin** basket on the counter and headed for the bathroom. As is my habit, I used too much **toothpaste**. I put on my **pajamas** and crawled into bed.*

Chair

The Nobel Museum (now the Nobel Prize Museum) was dedicated in 2001 to celebrate the one hundredth anniversary of the Nobel Prize. Within the museum, one of the most popular spots for visitors is the Bistro Nobel, designed to reflect the look and feel of a historic Viennese café. The bistro serves some of the same cuisine that Nobel laureates have been treated to over the years. For many visitors, however, the highlight of the experience is not the food but the chairs. It is common to see visitors wait to occupy a specific chair or even turn chairs over. Why? Because the bottoms of many chairs are signed by Nobel laureates.

Signing chairs dates to the museum's opening. One attendee at the opening was former US president Bill Clinton who, although not a Nobel Prize winner, decided on a whim to sign and date the bottom of a bistro chair. Instead of the signature being met with consternation, museum officials liked it and decided they should ask all Nobel laureates to sign a chair, thus beginning a new tradition.

Laureate Svante Pääbo (Physiology or Medicine, 2022) signing a chair at the Nobel Prize Museum in Stockholm. © Nobel Prize Outreach. Photo: Clément Morin.

Today, every new laureate must sign the bottom of a chair in the café. Laureates who received their prize before 2001 are invited to sign a chair if they happen to be in Stockholm. There are now hundreds of laureate signatures. Every signed chair is numbered, and you can ask for the key to the numbers. Of course, key or no key, no one is going to think you are crazy if they see you walking around turning chairs over.

Seashells

When Malala Yousafzai delivered her Nobel Peace Prize acceptance speech in 2014, she received a standing ovation that lasted well over a minute. That moment was remarkable on two accounts. The first was that, at seventeen years old, Malala was the youngest person ever to receive a Nobel Prize. The second was that she was able to hear the applause because of a medical breakthrough that involved a seashell.

A vocal advocate for the education of girls in Pakistan, Malala became a target of violence. In 2012, a man boarded her school bus, walked up to her, and shot her in the left side of her head. She lived, but her injuries left her with facial paralysis and hearing loss. Her hearing was restored via a cochlear implant, a medical procedure perfected by Graeme Clark nearly twenty years before Malala was born.

Early in his career, Graeme Clark decided to help those who were deaf. The cochlea, a spiral-shaped cavity containing tiny hairs for hearing, was the key. Prior research had focused on single electrode external stimulation of the cochlea, but Clark believed a better approach would be the use of multichannel electrodes that could be inserted directly into the cochlea, thereby eliminating visible external wires that might get infected. But how could one thread wires through a delicate spiral cavity that had three loops?

Grass and a seashell as inspiration for the cochlear implant.

The solution came to Clark while on vacation near Sydney, Australia. He noticed a seashell on the beach with the same spiral shape as a human cochlea. Nearby were clumps of grass. He started playing with individual blades of grass and found that the blades could readily be slipped into and through the spiral shape. The reason? Grass blades were flexible at the tip (for winding through the shell) and stiff at the base (for maneuvering into the shell). Clark realized this was how electrodes needed to be designed so they could reach the inner nerve endings.

The word *cochlea* got its name from the Greek word for snail shell (κοχλίας, kokhlias). It is fitting that a seashell turned out to be the source of inspiration that helped restore the hearing of a Nobel laureate.

Water

In 1988, French immunologist Jacques Benveniste created quite a stir when he published a scientific paper in *Nature* claiming that water retained a memory of any substance that had once been dissolved in it, even after the substance was no longer present in a water sample. This remnant memory, termed the "memory of water," allowed water to possess diagnostic and therapeutic properties beyond what mainstream science considered possible. Benveniste's work could not be reproduced and was categorized as fringe science.

Nearly a decade after the publication of the *Nature* paper, Nobel laureates Georges Charpak and François Jacob made comments about his work that Benveniste considered disparaging and that would lead the public to believe he had committed fraud. Benveniste filed a libel suit against Charpak and Jacob. A technicality derailed his chance at justice. A lower court dismissed the lawsuit, ruling that Benveniste had filed a civil suit and he should have filed a penal one.

Water was also a career ender for Luc Montagnier, one of the discoverers of HIV and a corecipient of the 2008 Nobel Prize in Physiology or Medicine. Montagnier read Jacques Benveniste's 1988 paper claiming that water had memory and became a believer. In 2009, Montagnier published a paper in a new journal in which he claimed that he could detect electromagnetic signals in water from bacterial DNA, even after extensive dilutions. The work was met with skepticism and was deemed nonreproducible. Still, Montagnier clung to this idea and made this research his new mission. He left France after receiving an offer to head his own institute in China, which of course bore his name. When he died in 2022, the journal *Science* wrote a nice thousand-word retrospective of his life and accomplishments. Only four words dealt with his ill-advised pursuit of electromagnetic water.

Refrigerator

In the classic movie *Back to the Future*, Dr. Emmett Brown, the wild-haired, absent-minded, and eccentric inventor and scientist, develops a time travel machine that uses a 1.2-gigawatt (1.2 billion watts) flux capacitor to convert garbage into power. Towards the end of the movie Emmett Brown uses a lightning rod to power the flux capacitor and save the world.

Now imagine a movie called *Einstein and the Killer Refrigerator*, where a wild-haired, absent-minded, and eccentric inventor and scientist – who also happens to be a Nobel laureate – tries to save the world from deadly appliances. Equally fantastical, except for the fact that this is a true story. Best known for his theory of relativity, Albert Einstein, the 1921 laureate in physics, had practical ideas as well. Einstein held multiple patents, one of which was for the Einstein-Szilard refrigerator.

Refrigeration was already around when Einstein was a young man, but refrigerators were killing people. The gases used as refrigerants at the time included carbon dioxide, sulfur dioxide, ammonia, and methyl chloride. These toxic gases would leak when the pump valves or seals of the mechanical compressors failed, causing the deaths of entire households while they slept. Albert Einstein and his colleague Leo Szilard designed a refrigerator that avoided the need for seals that could go bad. Instead of the mechanical pumps used in existing commercial refrigerators, the Einstein-Szilard refrigerator used an electromagnetic pump that required no moving parts.

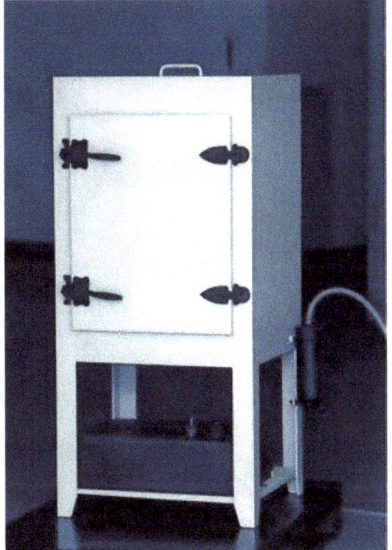

Working reproduction of the Einstein-Szilard refrigerator. Courtesy of the University of Oldenburg.

Einstein and Szilard received a US patent on November 11, 1930, for their invention. The electromagnetic refrigerator may have become the new standard for cooling but for a series of circumstances. The Great Depression hit, and financial institutions tanked. The venture capitalists who could have funded the optimization of the Einstein-Szilard refrigerator fell victim as well. The economic collapse in Germany aided the rise of Adolf Hitler.

German citizens such as Einstein and Szilard fled the country and had to start over. Equally important was the introduction in 1930 of the purportedly nontoxic chlorofluorocarbon Freon by the Kinetic Chemical Company, a joint business of Du Pont and General Motors. Introducing a new type of refrigerant was easier than introducing a new type of compressor.

Einstein held other patents for such things as a self-adjusting camera, an electrical sound system for a hearing aid, and an expandable blouse. Unfortunately, like the refrigerator, none of these inventions made it into commercial production. Poor Albert Einstein had to settle for receiving an appointment at Princeton University, being named *Time* magazine's Person of the Century, having a medical college named after him, and winning a Nobel Prize.

Yogurt

You might think that a scientist would be most remembered for the work that led to a Nobel Prize. Not so for Élie Metchnikoff (also known as Ilya Metchnikov). In 1908, Metchnikoff shared the Nobel Prize in Physiology or Medicine for his discovery of how white blood cells protect the body against diseases, a process called phagocytosis. Yet, in many parts of the world, people associate Metchnikoff with yogurt rather than a Nobel Prize.

In the 1880s, twenty years before receiving the Nobel Prize, Metchnikoff traveled around the Balkan peninsula, making notes on the lifestyles and cultures of the people. He was particularly struck by his observation that Bulgarian farmers and laborers had notably longer life spans compared to more affluent city dwellers. After investigating the numerous lifestyle factors that might account for this, he concluded that it was the yogurt (more specifically the Lactobacillus species in sour milk that converted sugar to lactic acid) that added years to the lives of these people.

Metchnikoff went on to propose that bad bacteria in the gut were the major contributors to a shorter life. Changing the gut bacteria composition to predominantly good bacteria might be the secret to routinely living well beyond a hundred years. Yogurt or other sour milk products were the simple route to achieve this goal. He wrote in the book titled *Scientifically Soured Milk: Influence in Arresting Intestinal Putrefaction*, "It is evident that the intestinal microbes are influenced by the food we eat. This variation of the intestinal microbes in its relation to our foods permits us to modify the intestinal flora by replacing harmful bacteria with those that are useful." His reputation made this unquestionably true. Interestingly, the book was published by the Lacto-Bacilline Company of New York, producers of Bacillac, the Metchnikoff Scientifically Soured Milk.

Metchnikoff toured Europe espousing the benefits of yogurt. His lectures created a frenzy over yogurt and the creation of a whole new commercial industry. Spaniard Isaac Carasso formed a company for large-scale manufacturing of yogurt, naming the company Danone after his son Daniel. Dannon yogurt is now a household name.

Left, Metchnikoff's book touting the benefits of soured milk. Right, a 1908 caricature making light of Metchnikoff's use of coagulum (clotted milk) in helping people reach 100 years (centenaires). Left, courtesy of WD Gann, Inc.; right, courtesy of Institut Pasteur/ Musée Pasteur.

Coin

There is a game show called *Who Wants to Be a Millionaire* that has been on television for decades. In this game, contestants try to answer multiple-choice questions that have increasing difficulty but also increasing prize money. The starting question is worth $100 and the final question, if a contestant gets that far, is worth $1 million. After winning money for a correct answer, the contestant faces a new question and has the choice of staying with their answer to the question, risking their winnings, or walking away with their earnings. They even get to see the four possible answers before deciding. The game show host also allows contestants to call a friend, remove two of the four answers, or ask the audience for their votes (the audience is usually correct). Yet long before the million-dollar question comes into play, most contestants walk away, even though the help of the audience, asking a friend, or eliminating two of the four answers puts the odds well in the contestant's favor. This is a phenomenon called loss aversion or Prospect Theory, in which a person prefers to avoid losses over equivalent or even larger gains.

Prospect Theory was developed in the 1970s by economists Daniel Kahneman (2002 Nobel Prize in Economics) and Amos Tversky, who died before he could receive the same prize. They performed an experiment that demonstrated a person's bias against losses. Tversky and Kahneman asked people if they would accept a bet that involved the flip of a coin. If the coin came up tails, the person would lose $100, and if it came up heads, they would win $100.

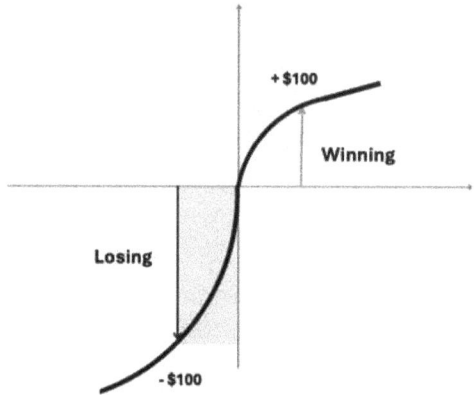

Loss aversion in Prospect Theory. The emotional pain felt by losing a coin flip is twice as strong as the pleasure felt by winning.

There were few takers. Why? Because the pain of losing $100 was greater than the pleasure of winning $100. What if Tversky and Kahneman upped the winning amount to $200? That seemed to change everything. People needed to gain about twice as much as they were willing to lose to consider accepting the bet. Tversky and Kahneman expanded this theory to show how it affects the global economy, even how it relates to selecting workers.

When they wrote their first paper for publication, Tversky and Kahneman flipped a coin to decide who would be the lead author.

Toothpaste

In 1945, Indiana University dental student Joseph Muhler discovered that stannous fluoride was an effective cavity-preventing chemical. Working with chemistry professors Harry Day and William Nebergall, the three demonstrated that toothpaste containing fluoride could reduce tooth decay by 50 percent. Out of this research, the first fluoride-containing toothpaste,

Crest, was launched in 1955. Today, fluoride toothpaste, rinses, and whiteners are standard tools in the armament against dental diseases. One might think that this was Nobel Prize caliber work, but not so. None of these scientists received a Nobel Prize, although in 2020, Indiana University dedicated a historical marker recognizing their contributions.

The link between toothpaste and the Nobel Prize has a most unlikely origin: Pierre and Marie Curie. The Curies shared the Nobel Prize in Physics in 1903 for the discovery of a natural process whereby atoms disintegrate and release ionizing radiation, a phenomenon that Marie Curie named "radioactivity." The element giving off this new form of energy was named radium. Pierre believed that radiation had great potential for curing cancer, which has subsequently proven true.

It was decades before scientists realized the hazardous nature of naturally occurring metals such as radium, polonium, and thorium. In the meantime, all people knew was that radioactivity meant energy, and people needed more energy added to their lives to maximize vim and vigor. Radioactive beauty products containing radium and thorium, such as toothpaste and face cream, hit the commercial market. In Paris, a Dr. Alfred Curie introduced Tho-Radia toothpaste, which contained the enamel hardening additives radium and thorium. Alfred Curie had no relation to the Nobel laureates Pierre and Marie Curie, but if the Curie name gave his toothpaste more credibility, Alfred was happy to let the public believe what it wanted.

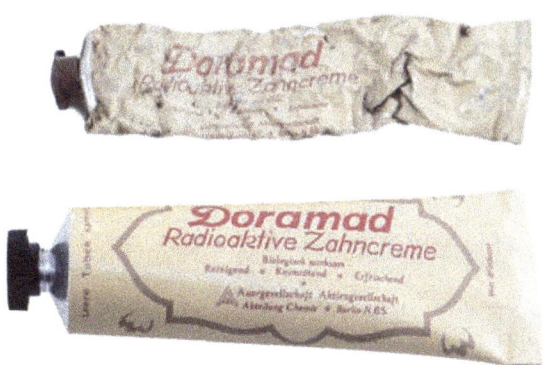

Doramad Toothpaste. The back label stated that the toothpaste's radioactive radiation increased the defenses of teeth and gums, loading the cells with new life energy that hindered the destroying effect of bacteria, yielding excellent prophylaxis and healing process with gingival diseases. Courtesy of Lucy Jane Santos, Museum of Radium.

The German company Auergesellschaft had a supply of thorium that was intended for military use. Diversifying its product menu, however, guaranteed another income stream. Deciding that a good use for its supply of thorium would be in personal care products, the company introduced Doramad toothpaste, claiming that its radioactive properties yielded superb prophylaxis and defense against gum disease.

Even the comedian Bob Hope got involved in the radioactive craze. On his radio show, *The Pepsodent Show*, Bob Hope endorsed Pepsodent toothpaste, which contained the powerful ingredient Irium. The public eventually found out that there was no such thing as Irium. Pepsodent's claims had no teeth behind them.

Pajamas

If you are a Nobel Prize winner, chances are good that you have had your picture taken in your pajamas. Possibly more than once. And you willingly went along with it.

The Nobel Prizes are announced each year starting on the Monday of the first full week in October. The official announcement is made at 11:00 a.m. Sweden time. Approximately forty-five minutes before the whole world has access to the name of the awardee, the Nobel Committee makes a telephone call to the soon-to-be-famous individual. The problem is the time zone differences around the globe. If the awardee lives in Europe, it is daytime. If the awardee happens to be an American, the phone call comes between 1:30 a.m. and 5:30 a.m. (a.k.a. the middle of the night). While the committee is wearing their best suits, the awardee is wearing pajamas.

More than once a family member has captured a photo of the occasion, pajamas and all, which has shown up on a Reuters feed or CNN. When Rainer Weiss received the call informing him of his Nobel Prize in Physics, he and his wife – as Weiss told *Boston Herald* reporter Jordan Graham – were sleeping and "quite nude." There appears to be no visual proof of their nudity. If there is a photo in existence, we've never seen it.

If the Nobel Committee is not successful in waking a prize winner in their pajamas when it calls in October, the Swedes get a second chance to create a Nobel pajama party two months later. Imagine being awakened by a knock on the door, groggily answering it in your pajamas, and seeing a young girl standing there. She is wearing a white gown and has a candle-lit wreath on her head. Not only that; she is accompanied by several other girls with candles as well as boys with cone-shaped hats and magic wands. All the girls sing a song for you. Then the girl with candles on her head offers to serve you breakfast in bed, which is a saffron bun with your choice of coffee or mulled wine. Other people, some of whom you recognize, appear and you find yourself a willing participant in a growing entourage strolling through the halls, watching others open their doors in their pajamas. No, this is not a wild dream. The girl is real. You are in your pajamas. You are at the Grand Hotel in Stockholm. It is December 13, and you are celebrating Santa Lucia Day in true Scandinavian style.

Literature laureate Imre Kertész and his wife being visited by Lucia in their suite at the Grand Hotel in Stockholm. TT/SIPA USA.

Held three days after the Nobel Prizes are awarded, Santa Lucia Day is a celebration of light in the world during the darkest days of the year. Honored on this day, St. Lucia was an early Christian martyr who fed the poor at night, often wearing candles on her head so she would have her hands free to carry food. Most Nobel laureates are still in Stockholm on December 13, winding down after several days of ceremonies, lectures, banquets, balls, and late-night celebrations of their own. Unless you are lucky, there's absolutely no escaping Santa Lucia Day. You might as well enjoy it. Besides, you get to see what fashionable nightwear other Nobel Prize winners own.

When the committee calls the next Nobel Prize winner, perhaps she will be in pajamas brushing her teeth before rinsing her mouth with water and heading to the refrigerator for Swedish yogurt, which she will enjoy while resting in an easy chair, thinking of seashells and the most revered coin in the world: the Nobel Prize Medal.

CHAPTER TWO

The Phone Call

Robert Laughlin's bedroom phone was apparently not working. Thirteen-year-old son Todd's phone, however, was working fine, and the unending noise was finally too much for even a teenager to avoid. Walking to his parent's bedroom, Todd told his dad that some guy from Sweden wanted to talk to him. At two o'clock in the middle of an October night, Robert Laughlin learned he had won the 1998 Nobel Prize in Physics through the speaker of a Mickey Mouse phone.

Laughlin's experience illustrates that, despite the Nobel Committee's best efforts, the process of contacting the recipient of a Nobel Prize doesn't always go as planned. Approximately forty-five minutes before the press release goes out identifying the newest prize recipient(s), the Nobel Committee makes a telephone call to the individual(s). It all goes well – if the Nobel Prize awardee answers her or his phone. That is where the wild card factors show up. Because of time zone differences, the awardee might be fast asleep or at the grocery store or traveling. The Nobel Committee may not have the correct phone number. Even if the call goes through, the awardee is told not to tell anyone until the Nobel Foundation makes the official announcement. All of which can lead to some interesting stories.

You Can't Tell Anyone

Richard Henderson was listening to a lecture being given by one of his group leaders when his phone rang. Given that he was in the middle of a crowded room and somewhat trapped, he rejected the call. He then noticed that the call was from Sweden. A second call came less than a minute later. Henderson decided that maybe it was important, and he should return the call. Repeatedly excusing himself as he worked his way through the aisles, Henderson noted the glares from his colleagues. How rude to leave the room to take a phone call. The call turned out to be a congratulatory one notifying him of his selection to receive the 2017 Nobel Prize in Chemistry. "Congratulations Professor Henderson," they told him. "You can't tell anyone for an hour." Uh-oh! Henderson needed to go back and listen to the rest of his group leader's lecture. How could he explain himself? Fortunately, one of the upcoming speakers, connecting the date and

Henderson's hasty departure from the room, became suspicious that something unusual was happening and took out his own mobile phone. It wasn't long before the Nobel press conference was on the big screen in the conference hall. Henderson was again the focus of attention as he tried to sneak back into the room. This time, however, he arrived to smiles instead of glares.

§

Barry Marshall and Robin Warren had become recognized for their discovery, in 1982, of *Helicobacter pylori* and its role in gastritis and peptic ulcer disease. Years went by, however, and a Nobel Prize seemed increasingly unrealistic. In fact, two decades had passed and Robin Warren was retired. Yet, the duo would have dinner at the Old Swan Brewery on the river below King's Park on the Monday evening each October when the Nobel Prizes were announced, always after five. Then came October 3, 2005. Marshall and Warren were working their way through a couple of beers. The waiter had just arrived with the fish and chips when Robin Warren's cell phone rang. The conversation started out fine but soon became weird.

Robin Warren taking the Nobel phone call. Courtesy of Barry Marshall.

"Congratulations Dr. Warren. You have won the 2005 Nobel Prize in Physiology or Medicine. You can't tell anyone for an hour. Also, perhaps you can help us with a problem. We can't find Barry Marshall."

"He's here at a pub with me. Should I tell him?"

"No, the rules are that you cannot tell anyone before the official announcement."

"Can I hand him my phone?

"Yes."

After a short pause. "Hello?"

"Dr. Marshall? Congratulations, you have been selected to receive the Nobel Prize."

"More beer!"

Barry Marshall (left) and Robin Warren (right) at the Old Swan Brewery. Courtesy of Barry Marshall.

Then the conversation got weirder. Learning that Marshall and Warren were already at a pub celebrating the announcement of the Nobel Prize, the committee wanted to know who had leaked the word to the two scientists that they had won the prize before the committee had a chance to call. After finally clearing up that the meeting at the pub was an annual tradition, the folks in Stockholm felt reassured that there was not a mole on the committee.

Flying High

Nobel Prize awardees have been on planes when the prizes were announced, finding out about their newfound fame in unusual ways. On an October night in 1991, Richard Ernst was flying from Moscow to New York.

Sleeping soundly, Ernst was awakened by the pilot telling him he had received an important telephone phone call. In 1991, calls were still being made on landlines, and no cord was long enough to reach thirty thousand feet in the air. Thinking it was unreal, Ernst mumbled something about clearly needing more sleep. No, the pilot insisted, Ernst had received a call, and he needed to take it in the cockpit. Minutes later, Ernst was wearing headset and communicating with the Nobel Committee, who informed him of his Nobel Prize in Chemistry.

Richard Ernst receiving the good news. Courtesy of ETH-Bibliothek Zürich, Bildarchiv.

§

Edvard Moser and his collaborator (and wife) May-Britt Moser were selected to receive the 2014 Nobel Prize in Physiology or Medicine. The committee successfully phoned May-Britt at her office, but she lamented that they could not get in touch with Edvard, who was flying to Munich and would not land until one in the afternoon. That was all the information needed to start a plan in motion. Moser got off the plane in Munich and immediately noted that something was strange. He was met at the gate – not at the baggage claim – by a young lady holding flowers and a name sign. Asked why she was there, the young lady responded that she did not know but it must be something good. As she escorted him to luggage claim, Moser checked his phone and noted nearly two hundred new emails or calls in the two hours he was on the plane. He also noted a call from Sweden. He then knew what the something good was.

§

Milton Friedman, recipient of the 1976 Prize in Economics, was on an early morning flight from Chicago to Detroit. He was to participate in a political event supporting an amendment to the Michigan constitution that might impact the people of the state. He was met at the airport by a small group of people close to the campaign. When the group arrived at the Press Center, there were reporters and photographers galore. A reporter ran up and asked what his reaction was to the award. "What award?" Friedman asked. Friedman was handed a teletype (look that word up if you want a history lesson) sheet that had been transmitted earlier that morning announcing his Nobel Prize. Friedman became famous. The amendment failed.

Relatives and Neighbors

As the sun was rising over Pittsburgh on October 11, 2021, octogenarians Stan and Sarah Angrist received a phone call from an unknown number from Florida. It was a reporter who asked to speak to their sixty-one-year-old son, Joshua, whom the caller claimed had won the Nobel Prize. Stan hung up. Since he was now awake, Stan checked the news on his computer. Indeed, the *New York Times* had announced that Joshua Angrist had been selected to share the Nobel Prize in Economics. Stan called his son and asked if he knew anything about the award. Kind of, his son replied. The parents' call confirmed the multitude of texts he had been getting. But he had slept through any calls if he had received them. In fact, Joshua was trying to find the telephone number for the Nobel Committee as the two spoke. Eventually, he was able to get the number from another Nobel laureate. The first time he called Sweden they wouldn't take his call. That very morning Joshua Angrist had planned on taking a final fall sailing trip to Cape Cod. Instead, the winds of fortune took him all the way to Stockholm.

§

Ardem Patapoutian, a neuroscientist at the Scripps Institute in California, turned on the Do Not Disturb setting on his phone each night so he could get some sleep. When the Nobel Committee tried to call him at two in the morning, there were no ringing, vibrating, or ping notifications that Ardem had missed a call or text message. Somehow (likely from Patapoutian's nomination packet), the committee ascertained that Ardem's 94-year-old father, Sarkis Patapoutian, lived nearby in Los Angeles. Calling the senior Patapoutian in the middle of the night, the committee got doubly lucky. Not only did the man answer, but Sarkis could also get through to his son because his son's iPhone had a Favorites setting where authorized people could bypass the Do Not Disturb feature. Just a few minutes before the rest of the world heard the official announcement, son Ardem heard from his father that he had won the 2021 Nobel Prize in Physiology or Medicine.

§

Neighbors get roped in as well. When Stanford University professors Robert Wilson and Paul Milgrom won the Nobel Prize in Economics in 2020, the Nobel Committee was able to get through to Wilson, who answered his phone at 1:30 a.m. The committee could not get through to Milgrom, who had his phone on silent mode. The solution turned out to be a rather simple one. The two colleagues lived across the street from one another. So, Robert Wilson and his wife, both wearing pajamas, walked across the street and rang and rang his neighbor's video doorbell until Milgrom finally answered. A groggy "hello" was followed by "It's Bob Wilson. You've won the Nobel Prize."

Robert Wilson did not wake up Paul Milgrom's wife, Eva Meyersson Milgrom. Eva was already awake because she was nine time zones and 5400

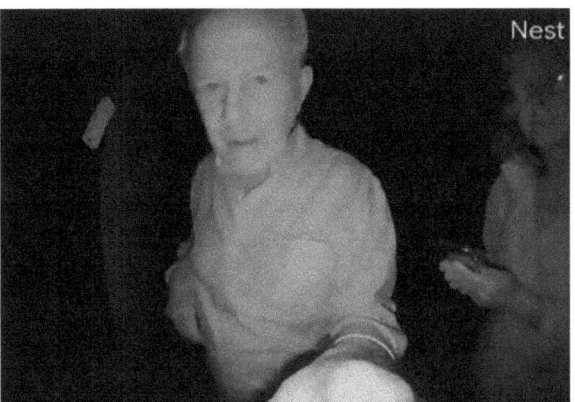

Robert Wilson (with wife) ringing the doorbell at the Milgrom household at 2:15 a.m. on October 12, 2020. Courtesy of Paul Milgrom.

miles away in Stockholm, the very city from which the Swedish Academy was trying to reach her husband. Eva received a security-camera notification on her phone. She saw her neighbor on the camera and got to watch live as Wilson told her husband he'd won the Nobel Prize.

Sorry, Wrong Number

Norman Ramsey shared the Nobel Prize in Physics in 1989. But he was not the first Norman Ramsey to hear about it. There was a Norman Ramsey in Washington, DC, and the Nobel Committee assumed that it was the esteemed physicist. Calling at 6:00 a.m., the committee asked the boy who answered if his father was home. Yes, he was, but he was sleeping. Could the committee speak to him? It was important since his father had just won the Nobel Prize in Physics. The boy responded that this was quite amazing since his father was an economist.

§

In 1998, the Royal Swedish Academy of Sciences made a transatlantic call to Los Angeles, asking the operator to connect them with Donald Cram. This was the beginning of a story that made Donald Cram a celebrity who ended up on *The Tonight Show Starring Johnny Carson*. At least, the Donald Cram who received the congratulatory call, not the Donald Cram who had truly won the Nobel Prize.

The operator said yes, there was one listing for Donald Cram, and put the call through. It was six o'clock in the morning in California and, like the call to Norman Ramsey above, a boy answered. At the Cram household, however, the call went way off course. Young Jonathan Cram went to retrieve his father, Donald O. Cram, telling him there was a man with an accent on the phone who wanted to speak with him. The caller said he was calling from Stockholm, to which Donald Cram said "sure" since he thought it had to be someone bombed at a bar. The caller claimed he was indeed from the Swedish Royal Academy of Sciences, and it was his pleasure to inform Cram that he had received the Nobel Prize in Chemistry. Now, Donald O. Cram did indeed have a degree in chemistry, which he used when he mixed chemicals for his carpet cleaning business. As Cram told the *Los Angeles Times* when the word got out, "Now, I do a good job on carpets, but this seemed a little excessive."

Carpet cleaner Donald O. Cram on The Tonight Show.
Courtesy of Carson Entertainment Group.

Donald O. Cram recounted the call on *The Tonight Show*. After a few minutes of confusing conversation with the person with the accent, during which Cram was having difficulty not laughing, he hung up the phone and went back to bed, still chuckling. His wife asked him who was on the phone, to which he replied, "I just won the Nobel Prize." Being a sweet wife, she responded, "That's nice."

Now, the story could have ended there, but it didn't. Ten minutes later the phone rang again. Same person, who tried to convince the carpet cleaner that he had won the Nobel Prize. At this point, Cram decided to play along, asking for which of his discoveries had he received the prize. The caller said that it was for his work on chemical and molecular recognition using molecules that mimicked substances found in nature. At this point, Donald O. Cram realized that this was too technical to have been made up by a prankster. It was time to fess up. "You mean Professor Donald J. Cram at UCLA. I'm just Donald Cram in Altadena."

Don't Ruin My Walk

Barbara McClintock also missed the call in October of 1983. McClintock made sure that she had quiet time each day. Thus, her colleagues at the Cold Spring Harbor Laboratory heard the news before McClintock did. When informed of the award, she simply responded "That's nice." McClintock was in no rush to get back to the office. She was picking black walnuts on the grounds, and if the press came calling, they could tag along and help her pick walnuts. Which they did.

Barbara McClintock (center) not letting journalists spoil her regular morning walk. Courtesy of the BGI Nobel Laureates Archives, Cold Spring Harbor Laboratory, NY.

You Can't Fool Me

Laureate May-Britt Moser, mentioned earlier, was finishing a meeting that ran too long and was rushing to her next meeting when her phone rang. She did not recognize the number but thought it might be important. She went to her office, where the caller identified himself as from the Nobel Committee. "Why are you calling me? Do you want some comment about another prize winner?" "No, it's you!" was the response. Not believing it, May-Britt Moser asked him to send an email to prove who he was.

§

Other Nobel Prize winners have been unconvinced that the call was real. James Mirrlees, who shared the 1996 Nobel Prize in Economics, did not believe the caller and insisted that the committee provide some other form of proof. John Gurdon, who received the 2012 Nobel Prize in Physiology or Medicine, thought that the caller had a fake Swedish accent and told the caller so. So did Toni Morrison when notified of her 1993 Nobel Prize in Literature. She demanded that the committee send her a fax to prove they were who they said they were.

§

And then there is David MacMillan and his $1,000 bet over the 2021 Nobel Prize in Chemistry. The bet was between two Nobel Prize winners who were 4,800 miles apart, one being in Amsterdam where it was 10:00 a.m. and the other in New Jersey where it was 4:00 a.m.

At Princeton, Professor David MacMillan's wife woke him and told him to turn his phone off because it kept buzzing. MacMillan saw a call from Sweden but knew it had to be a student playing a prank. Spam callers could make it look like any number or country was calling. He then noticed a text from Stockholm where his name had been spelled incorrectly as *Dr. McNillan*. More proof of Nobel-day mischief going on. MacMillan texted his collaborator, Benjamin List, to warn him, then went back to sleep. Soon after, List, who was wide awake in Amsterdam and who had received the official call from the Swedish Academy, sent back a text stating "wake up :-)"

After receiving the text, MacMillan called List, who unsuccessfully tried to explain that he had received a phone call congratulating him on winning the Nobel Prize, followed by another call asking for MacMillan's phone number. Focusing on the second half of List's explanation, MacMillan now knew how a prankster had gotten his phone number. From List!

Benjamin List received two calls, the
second asking for David MacMillan's
phone number. Courtesy of Benjamin List.

MacMillan had had enough and bet $1,000 that List was wrong. Well, the
two had indeed won the Nobel Prize and MacMillan was going to be out
$1,000. MacMillan agreed to pay up but held off while deciding whether to
pay in pennies or use one of those big checks. In the end, the $1,000
exchanged hands. List, however, immediately gave it back to help fund a
scholarship program MacMillan had set up for disadvantaged students in
Scotland.

I'm a Schnook

In 2008, chemist Martin Chalfie received a call from Stockholm but slept
through it. The normal ring on his phone had been accidentally changed a
couple of days before and the new ring was quite soft. Chalfie woke up in
his New York residence at six in the morning and realized it was noon in
Sweden, where the Nobel Prizes had been announced several hours earlier.
Well, maybe next year, he thought. As he later told Adam Smith from
Nobelprize.com, Chalfie had wondered who the schnook was that won this
time: "And so I opened up my laptop, and I got to the Nobel Prize site and I
found out I was the schnook!" The now famous schnook ran to the bedroom
and told his wife: "It's happened." To which his wife replied, "What? Have
we overslept taking our daughter to school?"

CHAPTER THREE

Beyond the Grave

Everybody dies. Even Nobel Prize winners. The death of a Nobel laureate, however, merits press releases, front-page news stories, elaborate obituaries, fancy funerals with photographers, and worldwide headlines. No ordinary headstones for a member of this elite group. Top shelf all the way.

More often than would be imagined, Nobel laureates have not gone quietly into that good night – in a dignified manner. True egos have been revealed, bodies gone missing, family scandals come to light, lost loves reunited, even criminal investigations involved. I would go so far as to argue that some Nobel laureates have provided a more interesting story dead than alive.

The Obituary

"The Merchant of Death: Dr. Alfred Nobel, who became rich by finding ways to kill more people faster than ever before, died yesterday."

Alfred was quite upset when he read this in a French newspaper. It was bad enough that the obituary was a scathing review that overlooked the accomplishments of a scientist with more than three hundred patents. What was even more surprising was the fact that the "deceased," Alfred Nobel, was reading it while drinking his morning coffee!

Newspaper headline "Decede Le Marchand De La Mort" (The merchant of death dies). Courtesy of sculpture creator Alexey Leonov.

As it turned out, it was Ludvig Nobel, not Alfred Nobel, who had died. An unfortunate journalistic error had been made. But it was an error that would impact Alfred from that day forward. Nobel thought of himself as essentially a pacifist, believing that the power of explosives and the damage they could cause would deter countries from war, not be used by humans to kill each other. Did the world see the inventor of nitroglycerin and dynamite as an Angel of Death rather than a successful international businessman, philanthropist, and patron of the arts?

Alfred Nobel contemplating his life after reading his own obituary. Courtesy of sculpture creator Alexey Leonov.

Because of this erroneous obituary, Nobel spent his remaining years ensuring that his legacy would be positive and lasting. Alfred died (for real) in 1896, eight years after that fateful obituary. The opening of his will, which was drafted in 1895 and deposited in a Stockholm bank, came as a surprise to friends, family, and the same press that had derided him. Nobel left nearly 95% of his fortune in trust to establish what has now become the most highly regarded of international awards, the Nobel Prize.

Alfred was cremated and interred at Norra Begravningsplatsen (Northern Cemetery), one of Stockholm's oldest cemeteries. Above his ashes is a large obelisk that says nothing about the man, simply his last name: NOBEL. It is never too late, however, to add fitting words to a grave. I suggest, "Every man ought to have the chance to correct his epitaph in midstream and write a new one." These self-reflective words are from Alfred Nobel.

Who's Buried in Alfred Hollis's Grave?

Alfred Hollis never won a Nobel Prize. In fact, he was unknown except to his family and friends. Yet, Hollis might be buried in a grave with the headstone of a Nobel laureate above him.

On January 28, 1939, Alfred Hollis passed away in Menton, France, while sitting in a hotel lounge with a martini in his hand. He was a bachelor who never held a job and liked to live the good life traveling with his sister, Amelia Emery, and her husband, Albert. Nine of his siblings had previously died from tuberculosis and Alfred was next in line. He had long suffered from spinal tuberculosis and was forced to wear a steel surgical corset. Amelia arranged for burial at the cemetery in nearby Roquebrune. The selected location had a ten-year renewable lease, a common practice at that time. She and Albert were the only two attendees at brother Alfred's funeral. His body was so malformed by the disease that he needed to be buried in his corset to fit in a casket.

Alfred Hollis. Courtesy of Louise
Foxcroft and the Hollis family.

On the same day, William Butler Yeats, recipient of the 1922 Nobel Prize in Literature, also passed away in Menton. Yeats's wife, George, and his mistress, Edith Shackleton Heald, took turns keeping him comfortable that night. Also present at his deathbed was bisexual poet and Duchess of Wellington, Dorothy Wellesley, with whom Yeats also had a relationship. And that's the normal part of this story.

Yeats, who had personal ties to County Sligo, Ireland, had the opportunity to be buried there. However, he asked that his body not be returned immediately but be placed in a temporary grave in Roquebrune, France, and then later returned to a final resting place in Drumcliffe churchyard in Sligo. He instructed George, "If I die, bury me up there [the Roquebrune churchyard] and then in a year's time, when the newspapers have forgotten me, dig me up and plant me in Sligo." George also took a ten-year lease on a grave, with a goal of returning the famous poet's body to Ireland in a year or two.

William Butler Yeats, 1911. Photo by Charles Beresford, National Portrait Gallery, public domain. PD-US.

The two men ended up in adjacent graves with simple marble slabs bearing their names and dates, one body to remain there for a long time, the other to have a brief respite before moving on. World War II, however, prevented George Yeats from carrying out her husband's instructions. It also prevented Amelia Emery from visiting the resting place of her brother.

In 1947, Amelia, along with other members of the family, made a pilgrimage to visit her brother Alfred's grave. To their surprise, the section of the cemetery where his body had been laid to rest had vanished. Seeking an explanation from local officials, they were told that numerous graves in that section had been disturbed and the remains moved to an ossuary. Officials would normally be happy to look at their files and clear up any questions, but all burial records had been lost or moved somewhere in the fog of war.

Yeats's and Hollis's adjacent graves in Roquebrune, 1939. Courtesy of Louise Foxcroft and the Hollis family.

That same year, Yeats's last mistress, Edith Shackleton Heald, along with her new companion, Hannah Gluckstein, traveled to France to see her dearly departed lover. Unable to find the grave, the two women sought answers. The person who had overseen exhumations vaguely remembered Yeats because his body was wrapped with a circular steel surgical truss. This set off alarms with Heald since the Yeats did have a hernia but had worn a simple leather truss, not the steel device described by the cemetery official. Who could have worn a steel surgical corset?

In spite of the questionable handling of graves at the cemetery, George Yeats began the process of returning the poet's body to Ireland. After negotiations between the Irish and French governments, the process was set in motion. Later investigations, however, have suggested that, at best, only some of the contents belonged to William Butler Yeats. The remainder more likely belonged to Alfred Hollis. According to records obtained from French diplomats, both governments knew that it was nearly impossible to return the complete remains of Yeats. Officials even went so far as to ask the local pathologist in charge to reassemble a skeleton that had the characteristics of the Irish poet. In the certificate of exhumation, the pathologist used the presence of a thoracic corset as the starting point for reassembling Yeats's skeleton. Yeats did not wear a thoracic corset, but Alfred Hollis did. Independently, the original physician who had attended both Yeats and Hollis when they died recalled instructions that the body with the steel corset was the one to be exhumed.

Undertakers screwing down the lid of the outer coffin containing Yeats's body. Private collection of Jack Millar, File ACC2021-02-76. Courtesy of the Military Archives of Ireland.

Even the casket invited suspicion. It appeared shiny and new, nothing like a casket should look if it had been in the ground for nearly a decade. The plaque on the lid was pitted and its luster long gone, yet the screws used to anchor it were new. The French ambassador to Dublin wanted the honor guard escorting the casket to be prepared if the Irish officials asked questions about a new casket. Their answer was to be that this was done for safe transport to Ireland. The repatriation process also required that the coffin not be opened. The casket had been soldered shut to discourage Irish officials from investigating its contents. Documents discovered years later support the notion that many people involved in the process had a tacit understanding of the need for diplomacy over transparency, in the interest of foreign relations.

Kids used to ask their friends, "Who is buried in Grant's tomb?" as a way of mocking their intelligence. Obviously, Grant was buried there. Well, what about poet and Nobel laureate William Butler Yeats? Who is buried in Yeats's grave? If you answered Yeats, you may want to think again. And what about this story? Is it a tale of finding a Nobel laureate and losing an unremarkable man, or of finding an unremarkable man and losing a Nobel laureate? Perhaps it's a tale of poetic injustice.

Only Strong Pallbearers Need Apply

Like William Butler Yeats, Marie Curie and her husband Pierre were also buried twice. Like Yeats, both Marie and Pierre were disinterred from their original grave sites and transported with honor guards and pomp and circumstance to their new resting places. Like Yeats, special precautions were in place when the bodies of Marie and Pierre were exhumed. But there was one major difference. While Yeats's casket was specially soldered shut to protect the poet from the public, Marie and Pierre's caskets were altered to protect the public from the Curies. The scientists were radioactive.

The Curies and Henri Becquerel shared the 1903 Nobel Prize in Physics for the discovery of a natural process whereby atoms disintegrate and release ionizing radiation, a phenomenon that Marie Curie named "radioactivity." Pierre believed that radiation had great potential for curing cancer, which has subsequently proven true. But before Pierre could do further research into the positive effects of radiation, he was killed in 1906 by a wagon while crossing a Paris street. Pierre was likely already showing signs of radiation exposure, but these were not recognized at the time. At a simple ceremony, Pierre was laid to rest in the family plot at Sceaux, France, outside of Paris.

Marie continued her research, winning another Nobel Prize in Chemistry in 1911, the first person to win two prizes. Marie suspected that her work came with a potential risk to her health, but no one at the time understood the true hazards of radiation. She continued working in the laboratory, finally succumbing to aplastic anemia in July of 1934. On July 6, she was interred in the same cemetery in Sceaux where her in-laws and Pierre lay.

In 1994, French President Francois Mitterrand decided that Marie Curie's body belonged in the Pantheon, alongside the likes of Voltaire, Jean-Jacques Rousseau, and Victor Hugo. If Mitterrand could achieve this, Marie would be the first woman to be buried at the Pantheon based on merit. Mitterrand contacted Marie's daughter, Eve Curie, with the good news about the special recognition being offered to this famous French woman. Unfortunately, he made one crucial mistake. Mitterrand neglected to consider that Marie had been part of a scientific duo (both in love and career) that included her husband, a Nobel laureate in his own right. What about Pierre's remains? Oops. Sensing a hidden agenda behind why the French President was eager to only honor Marie, daughter Eve declined the reburial of her mother in Paris. After a second conversation the following year, where there was an emphasis on honoring the famous couple, enshrinement at the Pantheon received the go-ahead.

As with most stories, there is almost always a "but" or a "however." In this case it was the very thing for which the Curies had become famous: radioactivity. The bodies might still be emitting radiation. Bearing this in mind, and with precautions in place, the excavation of Marie and Pierre was initiated in April 1995. Marie's grave was first. As the workers made it all the way to the wooden coffin, the radiation levels were not much above the background levels obtained from the surrounding area in the cemetery. Upon opening the lid of the coffin, the workers understood why. They were now looking at a separate, intact lead coffin about an inch thick. Inside that coffin was a remarkably preserved, but also radioactive, Marie Curie. Next came the exhumation of Pierre, who died nearly thirty years before Marie and had been in the ground for ninety years. Pierre's remains had surprisingly high radiation levels.

Once back in Paris, the Curies were placed in identical caskets specially made to fit into the niches at the Pantheon. These caskets were also lined with lead, which added an additional half-ton to their overall weight. The six French soldiers who carried the caskets earned their Pastis that day.

Pall bearers carry caskets with the remains of scientists Marie and Pierre Curie to be buried in the Pantheon, April 20, 1995. REUTERS/Pool New/Bridgeman Images.

If you wish to go to Paris and pay your respects to Marie and Pierre Curie, you can be thankful for two things. First, you were not a pallbearer recruited to carry the Curies' caskets. Second, you do not have to sign a waiver and wear a hazmat suit.

The Nomadic Life of Einstein's Brain

If you want to visit Albert Einstein's grave, you are out of luck. He has no grave. When he died, the 1921 Nobel laureate left instructions for his body to be cremated and his ashes spread at an undisclosed spot in the Delaware River. He wanted no publicized event that could end up as a circus with press and groupies running around. You cannot visit Einstein's grave. You can, however, visit his brain.

A trip to the Mütter Museum in Philadelphia will allow you to see forty-six slices of brain tissue belonging to Albert Einstein. They were donated by a neuropathologist, who got the slides from someone else, who got them from someone else, who got them from a pathologist named Thomas Harvey. And it is with Thomas Harvey that this story begins.

Einstein died at Princeton Hospital on April 18, 1955. He had a ruptured aortic aneurysm, a condition so grave that surgery would have given him only a small chance of recovery. He died with his family at his side. His body was transferred to the morgue where, in the basement of a hospital, the lives of Albert Einstein and pathologist Thomas Harvey would become forever linked. A simple autopsy was to be performed for the purpose of confirming the cause of death. Thomas Harvey, the pathologist on call, went way beyond any required evaluation of Einstein's chest and opened Einstein's cranium to look at the brain of this genius. Succumbing to temptation, and without the family's approval, Dr. Harvey removed the brain and took possession of it. He also removed Einstein's eyeballs and presented them to Henry Abrams, Einstein's ophthalmologist, who stored them in a safety deposit box somewhere in New York.

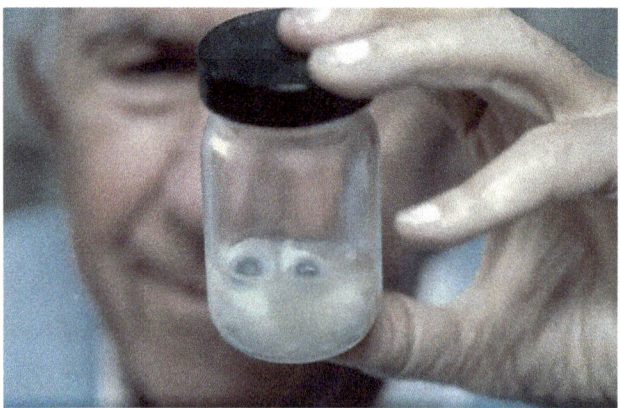

Ophthalmologist Henry Abrams at home with a container holding Albert Einstein's eyeballs. Michael Brennan Photography.

Henry Abrams died in 2009. His obituary made note of his long-standing doctor-patient relationship with the Einstein family but failed to mention Einstein's eyeballs.

Within a short period of time, Thomas Harvey was dismissed from Princeton Hospital for not only removing Einstein's brain without permission, but also for refusing to return it. After confessing to having extracted the brain, Harvey claimed he had obtained permission from Albert Einstein's son, Hans, to safely store it and only use it for valid medical research. That flimsy excuse did not fly, and his career was over. Harvey took the brain to Philadelphia where he somehow arranged for a part of the brain to be sliced into roughly 240 pieces and preserved for other medical researchers to use.

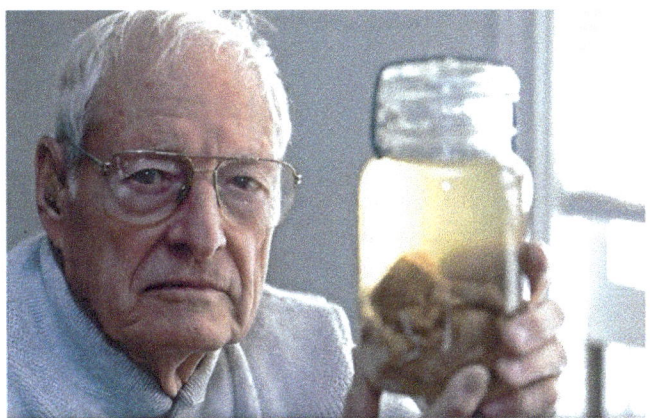

Pathologist Thomas Harvey holding a jar containing a portion of Einstein's brain. Michael Brennan Photography.

Harvey's marriage began to fall apart. The pathologist's wife threatened to toss the brain into the trash; Harvey decided to keep the brain and toss the wife. Over the next several decades Harvey found several jobs and carried the brain with him. In 1978, a young reporter named Steven Levy tracked down Thomas Harvey to Wichita, Kansas. After being asked if he had any pictures of Einstein's brain, the good doctor instead retrieved a cider box that was under a beer cooler. In the box was a glass jar containing Einstein's brain.

Being a nomadic brain, it continued its travels all the way to California. In 1997, Michael Paterniti, author of *Driving Mr. Albert*, again located Thomas Harvey, who was no longer in Wichita. Perhaps in a moment of remorse or perhaps wanting to rid himself of the brain once and for all, the eighty-five-year-old eccentric stated that he wanted to deliver the brain to Evelyn Einstein, Albert's granddaughter. So, with the jar of brain inside a Tupperware container, inside a duffle bag, inside the trunk of a Buick Skylark, the journalist and the pathologist drove across the country to Berkeley, where they met Albert's granddaughter, Evelyn, and showed her the brain. Evelyn had no real interest in an apology for how the brain had been treated, nor did she have any interest in keeping the brain. Back in the car it went.

In 1998, at the age of eighty-six, Thomas Harvey finally parted with Einstein's brain, donating it back to the Princeton Hospital. After fifty years of traveling the country, the brain of the man who brought us $E = mc^2$ returned home to the same hospital where its journey began.

Buried, Exhumed, Reburied, Exhumed, Reburied . . .

Chilean poet Pablo Neruda, winner of the 1971 Nobel Prize in Literature, holds the unique record as the only laureate to be buried three times. Pablo Neruda was exhumed twice, the second time as part of a criminal investigation.

Following his death in 1973, Neruda was originally laid to rest in Santiago. The poet's body, however, was exhumed in 1992 and reburied next to his wife Matilde Urrutia in the garden of their home in Isla Negra. This should have been the end of the story, except for one critical fact – the official cause of death was wrong. The medical records at the clinic where he died listed Neruda's death as resulting from a cancer-related wasting sickness known as cachexia. The truth was quite different.

The saga began with the 1973 military coup in which General Augusto Pinochet ousted Salvador Allende, head of the democratically elected Chilean government. Like many poets and authors, Neruda was active in the politics of his home country and was highly respected as a voice of the people. He was also a friend of Allende, who supposedly committed suicide at his home during the coup. Pablo Neruda was in the Chilean capital of Santiago receiving treatment for prostate cancer at the same time. During one clinic visit, Neruda took an unexpected turn for the worse, dying on September 23, 1973, only twelve days after Pinochet took power. Neruda was a national hero, but the new government banned any state funeral and made sure that he was buried at the Cementerio General (Santiago General Cemetery) within forty-eight hours. It took twenty years and the end of

Pinochet's rule for Pablo Neruda's body to be exhumed and returned to his home at Isla Negra.

Pablo Neruda's grave at Isla Negra, 2003. Courtesy of photographer Ricardo Mouat.

Immediately following his death, rumors circulated that Pinochet had arranged for Neruda to be assassinated while he was at the clinic. His primary symptoms on the day Neruda died were consistent with a urinary tract infection, not end-stage cancer. Something unusual had happened that day at the clinic. It remained a mystery until 2011, when Neruda's personal assistant and driver, Manuel Araya, came forward claiming that Neruda had called him on the day he died stating that he had received an odd injection in his stomach and now had a high fever. Neruda died a few hours later. Out of fear, the assistant had kept his secret for nearly forty years. Medical records revealed that Neruda was overweight at the time of his death, not wasting away. Adding to the suspicions was the history of assassinations that Pinochet had surely ordered during his time in rule. Most notable was the 1982 murder of former President Eduardo Frei Montalva, which had disturbing similarities to Neruda's death. The former president died suddenly after a routine operation at the same clinic where Neruda had died. Adding to the intrigue, the convicted perpetrators included the same doctors and the same nurse who had treated Pablo Neruda in 1973.

In 2013, faced with enough evidence that Neruda may have been assassinated, a Chilean judge ordered that Pablo Neruda's body be exhumed once again so that forensic specialists could test the body for toxins. None were found, but Chilean officials continued to believe that a third party was responsible for Neruda's death. Subsequent forensic testing took on a new angle and identified what could possibly be a laboratory-grown bacteria related to *Staphylococcus aureus*, the most dangerous of the *Staphylococcus* genus. A sixteen-member panel ultimately concluded that the original cause of death was wrong. The evidence pointed to an infection.

In 2016, after more than three years of storage at a government facility and the return of body parts that had been tested at laboratories around the world, the same Chilean judge ordered that the Nobel laureate's body be returned to his family. Neruda was buried for the third time in April of 2016. Today, flowers at the site hide the scars from the soil being disturbed so many times. If one looks further, it is possible to see, on the rocks below, a bust of the poet gazing out at the ocean.

The bust of Neruda, below his grave, looking out to the ocean.
© Glenn Stuart Beatty 2019. Used with photographer's permission.

In his work *Nothing But Death*, the poet wrote, "There are cemeteries that are lonely, graves full of bones that do not make a sound." Pablo Neruda's bones may have been silent, but they ensured that Pablo Neruda had the last word.

Karma

Isaac Bashevis Singer, winner of the 1978 Nobel Prize in Literature, was a lady's man. He often had multiple lovers at the same time, including his second wife, Alma Wasserman Singer, whom he stole from a friend, Walter Wasserman. Isaac Singer was a great writer but otherwise fell short in many ways. Perhaps karma had the last word when it came to his final resting place.

Singer died in 1991 in Surfside, Florida, yet his body was returned to a cemetery plot overlooking a housing development in Paramus, New Jersey. More on that later. The burial did not go smoothly. First, Singer's headstone contained a typo. It stated that he had received the *Noble* Prize. When notified of the error, his wife Alma said to let it go. Second, Alma had neglected to complete payment on the plot. Her limousine was stopped as it left the cemetery and immediate payment was requested, presumably under the threat that Isaac's time in the cemetery could be short-lived. Check only, no credit card.

Now, back to the reason that Isaac Singer is buried 1,300 miles from Surfside, Florida, a place he loved and where he lived when he died. It turns out that Alma Wasserman Singer wanted to be buried near her daughter from her marriage to her first husband, Walter. Beth-El cemetery in Paramus was the home of the Wasserman family plot. The plot next to the Wasserman cluster was available and Alma purchased it. Alma died in 1996. In the end, Isaac Singer's headstone sits next to Alma's, whose headstone sits just a few feet from her first husband Walter's, whose headstone sits next to Walter's second wife.

CHAPTER FOUR

Luck and the Nobel Prize

According to writer Frank A. Clark, "It's hard to detect good luck – it looks so much like something you've earned." I like Clark's message. Even if one works hard and achieves success, hidden somewhere is a little luck. This holds true for Nobel Prize winners as well. They have worked hard, sometimes alone and under challenging circumstances. Hard work has not always been enough, however, and good luck has played a prominent role in paths to the Nobel Prize. And then there is bad luck, which has caused individuals who should have received recognition to be lost to history. Here are stories that illustrate how luck has been the difference between success and failure, or fame and anonymity.

The Lucky Discovery of Insulin

In early 1921, Frederick Banting and Charles Best began studies on pancreatic secretions and their effects on blood sugar in dogs. Their findings were considered so important that the Nobel Prize in Physiology or Medicine was awarded in 1923 for the discovery of insulin. The prize was not awarded to Banting and Best, but instead to Banting and John Macleod.

Special cable from October 25, 1923,
announcing Banting and Macleod as the Nobel
Prize recipients. Public domain. PD-US.

How this happened is a story of insulin and luck that included not just Banting, Best, and Macleod, but also individuals named Noble, Collip, Walden, and Krogh.

Frederick Banting was a struggling young surgeon in London, Ontario. Lacking money, he signed on as a teaching assistant at the University of Western Ontario. While preparing a lecture on the pancreas, Banting found a 1902 paper dealing with tying off the pancreas in animals and how the islet cells helped prevented sugar dysfunction in diabetes. This gave Banting the idea of isolating secretions from islet cells to relieve high sugar in the urine. He kept pushing this idea until his chairman told him to go and see John Macleod, an authority on carbohydrate metabolism at the University of Toronto.

Macleod's reception of Banting and his idea was lukewarm. Macleod believed that the liver exerted control over carbohydrates. Banting was also unknown in the carbohydrate field. Nonetheless, Banting got lucky that day. Macleod offered to let Banting come for several months and use his laboratory space. Perhaps it had something to do with Macleod's leaving for a three-month summer holiday. Macleod also offered a summer research position to one of two students, Charles Best and Edward Noble. The two tossed a coin to see who would help Banting. In what became the luckiest event in Best's career, he won the toss.

Fellow students and friends Charles Best (left) and Clarke Noble (right), circa 1920. Courtesy of the Thomas Fisher Rare Book Library, University of Toronto.

Before leaving, Macleod helped Banting and Best develop experimental protocols and proper surgical techniques. During Macleod's absence,

Banting and Best made remarkable progress showing that extracts of pancreatic secretions could decrease blood sugar. They named the not yet fully purified component in the extracts isletin (later renamed insulin).

Charles Best (left) and Frederick Banting (right) with the first dog treated with insulin, 1922. Courtesy of the Thomas Fisher Rare Book Library, University of Toronto.

Upon returning, Macleod arranged for Banting and Best to stay on. The three scientists began using cow pancreas (obtainable in larger quantities) to extract insulin, but the purity remained poor. By luck, there was a scientist in town on a sabbatical who was experienced in extraction techniques. His name was James Collip. Macleod invited Collip to join the group. Using alcohol, Collip determined that insulin stayed in solution at lower alcohol percentages while unwanted compounds precipitated out. At 90 percent alcohol, insulin precipitated out and could be collected in a much purer form. Collip's purification techniques allowed an attempt at treating a human. In January 1922, Collip's extract was successfully used to treat a boy who was dying from diabetes at a local hospital. Bolstered by this success, the team expanded insulin therapy to more patients and initiated clinical trials, with plans towards large-scale production of insulin.

Suddenly, Collip's protocol went haywire. The insulin yield was zero for some extracts. Macleod sought advice from Lilly Pharmaceuticals. By luck, a Lilly chemist named George B. Walden remembered something he had read years before from a scientist who worked at, of all places, a brewery. It

James Collip. Note the massive flasks used to prepare extracts. Courtesy of the Thomas Fisher Rare Book Library, University of Toronto.

involved using the right acidity (pH) when making beer. Beer tasted better when brewed at a higher pH. Walden tested the effect of pH and discovered that acidity was more important than alcohol percentage in the yield of insulin. James Collip had to account for multiple variables in the large-scale extractions and had not consistently controlled for the pH. Once Walden's solution to the problem was incorporated, the yield of insulin increased tenfold.

By late 1922, Banting, Best, Collip, and Macleod were celebrities. Yet only Banting and Macleod won the Nobel Prize. Perhaps Best's status as a student assistant dismissed him from serious consideration. Perhaps James Collip, a sabbatical invitee, was seen as a minor contributor.

The decision to award the Nobel Prize to Banting and Macleod also involved a Danish couple named Krogh, who themselves entered the picture due to luck. August Krogh, who won the 1920 Nobel Prize in Physiology or Medicine, was invited in early 1922 to give a series of lectures in the USA. His trip was delayed because his wife Marie, herself a noted researcher, had been diagnosed with maturity onset diabetes and was beginning treatment back home. His son also fell ill.

August and Marie Krogh. Courtesy of Novo Nordisk.

By fall the family was doing better and the couple set out for the US. At a dinner party in Boston, Marie Krogh was seated next to the famous diabetologist Elliott Joslin, who told her about the recent discovery of insulin in Toronto. Marie persuaded her husband to extend their trip and go to Toronto to learn more about insulin. Soon the couple was in Toronto as guests at the home of – who else – John Macleod, whom August Krogh subsequently nominated along with Frederick Banting for the Nobel Prize.

Lucky Encounters

In 1974, thirty-year old Michael Rosbash began working at Brandeis University. A lover of sports and rock 'n' roll, his research interests focused on genetics. That same year, thirty-year-old Jeffery Hall also began working at Brandeis University. He also loved sports and rock 'n' roll. His research interests were also in genetics. Unlike a lot of academics, however, their collaboration did not start in the usual way, namely, attending the same seminar or serving on the same thesis committee. It started on the basketball court. Rosbash and Hall played pickup basketball with graduate students and local workers. After one of their weekly games, Hall, who worked on fruit flies, mentioned in the locker room that he was interested in learning about genes that controlled fruit fly circadian rhythms (sleep-wake cycles). Rosbash responded that genes were what he studied in his laboratory. They joined forces and within two years had identified the gene that regulated circadian rhythms. In 2017, these two Brandeis professors were awarded the Nobel Prize in Physiology or Medicine along with Michael Young from Rockefeller University. When Hall received the call from Sweden at around five a.m., he was already awake. He could rarely sleep through the night and was typically up well before sunrise. Rosbash, on the other hand, was awakened by the phone on his nightstand. He was sound asleep, as he always was at five in the morning. That's circadian rhythms for you.

§

Lucky encounters do not happen only at sports venues. In the 1990s, if you wanted to access an older published paper, you had to go to the library, pull the printed version from the shelf, and take it to a separate area to make a photocopy. There was always a waiting line. To get through the experience, you often struck up conversations with people also waiting in line. It is one such conversation that lined up a Nobel prize. In 1998, Drew Weissman was finishing his first year as a faculty member at the University of Pennsylvania. A trained immunologist, he focused on finding better ways to create vaccines. He was interested in a molecule called messenger RNA, which carries information from DNA in a cell nucleus, where it is then used to make proteins, even in viruses. Weissman wondered if there was the potential to create vaccines based on this short piece of RNA.

At this same time, a Hungarian researcher named Katalin Karikó, who had recently lost her tenure track position at the same university due to a lack of funding, was struggling to find laboratory space and financial support. No grant agency wanted to fund her because she had this wild idea that a molecule called messenger RNA had value that just needed to be proven. The two scientists regularly encountered each other while waiting their turn at a photocopy machine. One day, Weissman told Karikó about how he wished to study messenger RNA in his laboratory but did not know where to start. Karikó shot back that this was exactly what she did. As the saying goes, the rest is history. In 2023, the two shared the Nobel Prize in Physiology or Medicine for their discoveries using nucleoside base modifications, which laid the foundation for the development of messenger RNA vaccines against COVID-19.

That old photocopy machine is long gone. Weissman and Karikó now run into a different problem: journalists want to photograph the two of them next to a copy machine. Good luck finding one. People can download archived documents on their personal computers rather than wait in line at the library. Kariko and Weissman's story makes one wonder what future Nobel Prize ideas might get lost as one sees the outside of a library more than the inside. Well, there is always the line at Starbucks.

§

Many years ago, the brokerage firm EF Hutton ended their television commercials by showing a crowd of people falling silent when the company's name was mentioned. The commercial would close with the slogan, "When EF Hutton talks, people listen." Fortunately, Harry Markowitz listened to a stockbroker and ended up performing studies that helped him win the 1990 Nobel Prize in Economics. In the 1950s, Markowitz was a graduate student at the University of Chicago and was struggling to find a topic for his dissertation. Seeking advice, Markowitz visited his advisor's office but was asked to wait in an outer room until his advisor was free. There was another visitor in the room. Striking up a conversation, Markowitz learned that the man was a stockbroker. The financier inquired about Markowitz's dissertation topic. Markowitz said he didn't have one. During the rest of the conversation something magical must have been said because, when young Harold Markowitz was called into his advisor's office, he excitedly announced that the man outside had told him to do his dissertation on the stock market. Markowitz went on to do just that and became famous as the father of modern portfolio theory. Perhaps the stockbroker worked for EF Hutton! After all, when he talked, Harry Markowitz listened.

§

Eugene (Gene) Fama's professors at Tufts University had encouraged him to apply to the University of Chicago's business school for graduate studies. Fama had applied to multiple schools and had been accepted by many, but by the spring he hadn't heard back from Chicago. So, he called the university, where the dean of students, Jeff Metcalf, answered. For some reason, Metcalf and his secretary were the only two people around that day.

There was no record of his application, Metcalf told Fama. Fama insisted that he had sent one in. Now, Metcalf could have told him to send another application and rid himself of the young caller. Instead, Metcalf queried Fama about his grades. Fama responded that his undergraduate grades at Tufts University were very good. Metcalf couldn't know if that was true or not, but he caught the name "Tufts." The University of Chicago just happened to have a scholarship for somebody from Tufts. Metcalf asked Fama if he was interested. Fama accepted on the spot.

Gene Fama not only did his graduate work at the University of Chicago, but he also spent his entire teaching career there, later winning the 2013 Nobel Prize in Economics. Fama always wondered what path his life would have taken if Jeff Metcalf had not answered the phone that day.

There is an adage that states, "I'd rather be lucky than good." If you doubt this, perhaps you should consider Gene Fama's article, "Luck versus Skill in the Cross-Section of Mutual Fund Yields."

§

In 2023, Swedish writer Aris Fioretos walked into the Nobel Prize Museum bearing a gift: a suitcase missing a strap that had seen better days. This suitcase had an amazing story, that of a young Jewish poet who caught the last plane out of Nazi Germany in May 1940.

Poet Nelly Sachs won the 1966 Nobel Prize in Literature. A marvelous thing given that she was once a week away from becoming an anonymous victim of the Holocaust. Like many Jews living in Germany in the 1930s, Sachs received a notice to report to a Nazi concentration camp. But a lucky encounter that occurred years earlier helped her and her mother escape the country. The encounter was with a person whom Nelly Sachs never did meet – a Swedish writer by the name of Selma Lagerlof.

Selma Lagerlof when she won the 1909 Nobel Prize in Literature. Photo by Aron Jonason. Courtesy of Mårbackastiftelsen/Nobel Foundation.

In 1909, Selma Lagerlof was the first woman to win the Nobel Prize in Literature. Nelly Sachs received a copy of Lagerlof's first novel, *Gösta*

Berling's Saga, for her fifteenth birthday. Sachs knew then that she wanted to be a writer. In 1921, Sachs finished her first book, which she sent to Lagerlof. A response soon arrived in which Lagerlof thanked Sachs for the lovely book and praised her literary talent.

Nelly Sachs as a teenager. Photographer unknown, Wikimedia Commons, public domain.

Lagerlof and Sachs continued to exchange letters, writing about their ideas for novels. All was good. Until suddenly it wasn't. One day a letter from Sachs took on a new and serious tone. Kristallnacht, the night when Nazis had smashed synagogues and Jewish-owned stores, portended a grim future for Sachs. Thirty-year-old Sachs made a personal plea to her eighty-one-year-old friend for help in escaping Germany. She needed support from abroad for the required paperwork. Lagerlof, who was now quite frail, managed to write a letter of recommendation. After nearly a year spent obtaining the necessary documents, Sachs and her widowed mother decided it was now or never if they were to have even a slim chance of leaving Germany for a new life in Sweden. On May 16, 1940, Sachs and her mother packed what few possessions they could and boarded the last plane from Berlin to Stockholm.

Sachs never had a chance to thank her Swedish guardian angel for saving her. Selma Lagerlof had died in March, never knowing that she had successfully helped Sachs escape the gas chamber.

The suitcase Nelly Sachs carried as she fled Nazi Germany in 1940.
Photo by Nanaka Adachi, © Nobel Prize Outreach.

§

And then there was the lucky encounter that helped to create the world's most famous prize. In 1876, thirty-three-year-old Bertha Kinsky, a governess for a wealthy family in Vienna, was seeking a solution to a rather delicate problem. Bertha had developed a romantic relationship with her employer's oldest child Arthur, and the von Suttner family was not happy. Arthur's mother read an advertisement that had been placed in a Paris newspaper: "A very rich, highly educated elderly gentleman, living in Paris, seeks a lady likewise of a mature age, with a good knowledge of languages, as secretary and to be responsible for the household." Arthur's Mother presented it to Bertha and told her to answer it. Bertha did so. The "elderly gentleman," she subsequently found out, was forty-two-year-old Alfred Nobel, the inventor of dynamite.

Nobel had placed the advertisement in the newspaper, likely as an entry towards finding a bride. Nobel found Bertha intriguing, hired her, and moved her to Paris. It lasted two weeks. Nobel left on business. Taking advantage of Nobel's absence, Arthur von Suttner, Bertha's true love, sent her a communication asking her to elope with him. Bertha was gone by the time Alfred Nobel returned. She and Nobel only saw each other two more times prior to Nobel's death twenty years later.

Despite their short time together, Bertha Kinsky (now Bertha von Suttner) and Alfred Nobel continued to write each other and developed an enduring bond, something remarkable given the distinctly different paths each pursued. Bertha became a leading peace activist, writing a globally recognized book (*Die Waffen nieder* [Lay down your arms]), starting the Austrian Peace Society, and organizing international peace conferences. Nobel expanded his factories' capacity for manufacturing dynamite and continued exploring other explosives that could be used in warfare. Not surprisingly, the letters between the two often discussed war and peace. Both believed in peace; von Suttner believed that peace was achievable only through cooperation and recognition of commonalities rather than differences. Nobel was skeptical that countries would willingly cooperate, believing instead that when weapons existed that could annihilate entire populations, countries would come to their senses and exist peacefully. In the end, Nobel came to realize that the power of the pen in achieving peace was likely mightier than the power of the sword.

Left, Alfred Nobel in a photograph from the mid-1860s. Photographer unknown. Right, thirty-year-old Bertha von Kinsky shortly before she met Alfred Nobel. Wikimedia Commons, public domain.

Nobel specified in his final will that his fortune be used to create prizes for individuals who had conferred the "greatest benefit on mankind" in the areas of literature, physiology or medicine, chemistry, physics, and peace. The prize for peace was to be given "to the person who shall have done the most or the best work for fraternity between nations, the abolition or reduction of standing armies and for the holding and promotion of peace congresses." It was as if the award was created with Bertha von Suttner in mind. Indeed, von Suttner was awarded the Nobel Peace Prize in 1905.

Lucky Experiments

If you or a friend have ever safely received a blood transfusion, you can thank Nobel laureate Karl Landsteiner. Prior to Landsteiner's experiments on blood groups, scientific thought was that transfusion reactions resulted from some pre-existing disease in the patient or donor. Landsteiner was unconvinced that diseases were the cause. In 1901, he published the results from a seminal study on blood types that won him the 1930 Nobel Prize in Physiology or Medicine. Landsteiner had tested the agglutination (clumping) of blood from six of his colleagues depending on whose blood was mixed with whose. Clumping of someone's blood could kill them, so knowing the type of blood people gave or received was crucial. The 1901 publication described three types of blood – now called types O, A, B – that were evenly distributed among the six study participants. Landsteiner's demonstration of three blood types was a scientific advancement. But it was also the result of luck.

Sera	Blood corpuscles of:					
	Dr St	Dr. Plecn	Dr. Sturl	Dr Erdh	Zar.	Landst.
Dr St	−	+	+	+	+	−
Dr. Plecn	−	−	+	+	−	−
Dr. Sturl	−	+	−	−	+	−
Dr Erdh	−	+	−	−	+	−
Zar.	−	−	+	+	−	−
Landst.	−	+	+	+	+	−

Results from Landsteiner's 1901 paper. + meant that clumping occurred. Dr. St's and Landst's blood (type O) did not react with any other blood. Dr. Pleen's and Dr. Zar's blood (type A) did not clump with two other participants, and Dr. Sturl's and Dr. Erdh's blood (type B) did not clump with two other participants. (Landsteiner, "On Agglutination Phenomena of Normal Human Blood," *Wiener Klinische Wochenschrift* 14 [1901]: 1132–1134.)

Landsteiner and the five colleagues he grabbed from the laboratory happened to be different from the general population. Landsteiner's group was 33% type O, 33% type A, and 33% type B. The general population of Western Europe was 43% type O, 42% type A, and 11% type B, with the remaining few 4% type AB (when Landsteiner's group tested larger numbers of individuals, they subsequently identified type AB). With just six subjects, the probability that Landsteiner should have seen a single type B individual was 50/50 at best, the same as a coin flip. The probability that he would have seen two type B individuals was only 7%, far below the 33% for himself and his colleagues. Effectively, Landsteiner could have gone out and grabbed six people off the street and never have identified three blood types.

§

Smoking in a laboratory is not recommended. You might be unlucky and blow yourself up. For Otto Stern, however, smoking in a laboratory led to the lucky break he needed on his way to a Nobel Prize.

In 1922, Stern and colleague Walther Gerlach set out to test the two prevailing theories of the structure of the atom. In Niels Bohr's model, electrons moved in discrete orbits and directions around a nucleus in a magnetic field (like planets revolving around the sun). In the other model, electrons could be oriented any which way in a magnetic field. To prove which model was correct, Gerlach, with Stern's guidance, created an apparatus that would shoot a concentrated beam of superhot vaporized silver through a nonconsistent magnetic field, after which the silver atoms would deposit on a tiny glass plate. If Bohr's model was correct, the electrons in the silver atoms would move in only two directions (think up or down) under the influence of the magnet, and two lines of deposited silver would be observed. If the other model was correct, the magnetic field would cause the electrons to randomly scatter, with silver deposited in a blob shape.

Gerlach worked into the wee hours performing the experiment. He looked at the glass plate and saw no silver deposit on it. He called Stern over and gave him a "What happened?" look. Stern, who had his ever-present cigar in his mouth, saw nothing on the plate. Puffing away, Stern leaned in close

Otto Stern smoking a cigar in his laboratory. Courtesy of
AIP Emilio Segrè Visual Archives, Segrè Collection.

to figure out why the plate looked blank. As his smoke-ladened breath hit the plate, something weird began to happen. The trace of the beam began to appear and got darker. Two lines appeared.

It suddenly dawned on the duo what was going on. A layer of silver had been deposited just like planned, but it was too thin to be seen by the naked eye. The sulfur in the cheap cigars Stern smoked had reacted with the silver on the plate to create silver sulfide, a jet-black substance. The cigar smoke had acted as if it were a developing solution used to produce photos on film. The two lines confirmed Niels Bohr's model of the atom. Although it must have pained Gerlach to admit that Niels Bohr's directional quantization model was indeed correct, Gerlach sent Bohr a congratulatory postcard on February 8, 1922, which showed the results from the now-famous experiment.

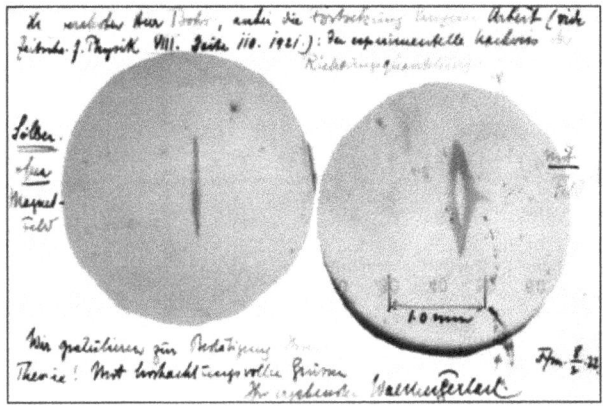

February 8, 1922, postcard from Gerlach to Bohr showing a photograph of the beam-splitting results. Courtesy of Niels Bohr Archive, Copenhagen.

Gerlach moved on to another professional position. Stern continued to refine his beam techniques, winning the 1943 Nobel Prize in Physics. With the money he received for his prize, Stern could have refined his taste in cigars. Likely not. There may be nothing like a good cigar paired with a fine whiskey, but there's also nothing like a cheap cigar paired with a Nobel Prize.

§

If you've ever used sticky tape to remove lint from a piece of clothing, you can relate to the lucky experiment in which sticky tape pulled from the trash helped solve a decades-old problem. Graphite, the material used as the "lead" in pencils, is crucial for producing batteries, brake linings, and lubricant powders. It also has high electrical conductivity and heat resistance. Graphite is made up of layers of graphene, which consists of single layers or sheets of carbon atoms arranged in a honeycomb pattern. Graphene is two hundred times stronger than steel, yet at the same time flexible and lightweight. The potential of graphene was massive if only someone could figure out how to make thin graphite films, ideally as thin as a one-carbon atom layer.

No one had succeeded until 2004, when Andre Geim decided to give it a shot in his laboratory. Geim gave a graduate student a thin disc of graphite and told him to grind and polish it down to a thickness of a human hair. He was able to get the disc down to a thickness of ten micrometers, not bad considering this equaled less than one thousandths of an inch. But it was still too thick by a factor of a thousand.

Oleg Shklyarevskii, a fellow working in another area of the laboratory, asked why they were wasting their time trying to grind down graphite. He stepped away for a few minutes and returned with some crumpled up sticky tape that had black dust on it. Shklyarevskii's area of expertise was scanning tunneling microscopy, for which he used graphite as a standard for instrument calibration. He would clean the surface of the graphite with tape, which was then tossed in the trash. Geim looked closely at the surface of the tape and saw tiny flakes of graphite many times smaller than he had seen before. By taking a fresh piece of tape, applying it against the surface of the other piece, and peeling it apart, the graphite layer got thinner on each piece of tape. Repeat, and the layers became progressively thinner, down to 10 nanometers thickness, now billionths of an inch. As Andre Geim claimed in the Nobel Price lecture, "Polishing was dead, long live Scotch tape!"

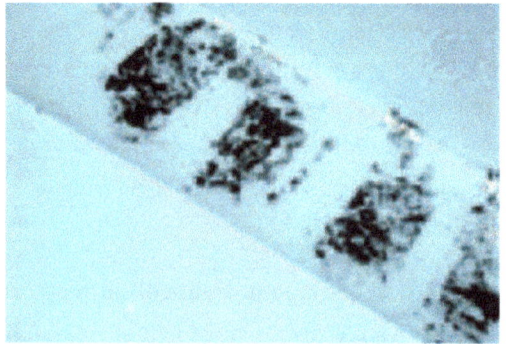

Remnants of graphite left attached to sticky tape. Credit:
Andre Geim Nobel Lecture, courtesy of Andre Geim.

Working with a student, Konstantin Novoselov, Geim kept improving techniques for isolating graphene. The initial manuscript describing their experiments was rejected by the journal *Nature* for not constituting a sufficient advance. Geim and Novoselov's contributions were, however, considered important enough to land them the 2010 Nobel Prize in Physics.

Graphite, graphene transistor, and sticky tape dispenser used for the exfoliation of single-layer graphene from graphite in 2004. Donated by Geim and Novoselov to the Nobel Prize Museum. Photograph by Gabriel Hildebrand, Wikimedia Commons, public domain.

When Geim and Novoselov visited Stockholm to receive the prize, they brought along a little souvenir for the Nobel Prize Museum to mark the occasion. A tape dispenser.

CHAPTER FIVE

Wayward Medals

Every December, in a formal ceremony, each Nobel Prize winner approaches the stage and receives a specially inscribed gold medal from the King of Sweden. There is a period of applause and photographs. Then something unusual happens. The gold medal is immediately handed back. Why? Because that evening, there is an extravagant banquet attended by hundreds of invited guests. Along with entertainment and libations, there is an after-dinner dance. One would not want to lose a Nobel Prize medal and not remember what happened to it. The next morning – or perhaps afternoon, depending on the amount and length of partying the night before – the laureates make their way to the Nobel Foundation offices to permanently claim their medals and diplomas. At least while everyone is in town, the medals are safe.

Well, not always. After Médecins Sans Frontières (Doctors Without Borders) received the 1999 Nobel Peace Prize in Oslo, the group celebrated with an evening of partying, during which the gold medal mysteriously vanished. Not even twenty-four hours had passed, and the medal was gone. Fortunately, the next day the gold magically reappeared in the suite at the hotel. Strangely enough, there were bite marks on it, adding to the mystery. It turned out that some members of the Médecins Sans Frontières delegation had taken the medal on a pub crawl around Oslo as a conversation opener (a.k.a. a pickup tool). Which answered two questions. Yes, gold was soft enough to make a tooth impression. No, a Nobel medal did not attract guys and chicks.

This is not the only unusual thing that has happened to these one-of-a-kind treasures. Some medals have been stolen. Two medals apparently vanished yet were still in plain sight. Medals have accidently ended up in the wrong Nobel laureate's hands. One medal was nearly confiscated at an airport. Others have been auctioned for both noble and not so noble reasons. All of which show that truth can be stranger than fiction.

I Think You Have My Medal

The Nobel medals given out in Sweden (Chemistry, Physiology or Medicine, Physics, Literature) are engraved with the laureates' names on the visible flat surface. The two medals presented in Norway (Peace, Economics) are different, with the laureates' names etched into the edge, a space not visible when the medals lie flat in their presentation cases. Sometimes small differences have large effects. In 1975, Leonid Kantorovich and Tallying Koopmans shared the Nobel Prize in Economics. Their medals were mixed up and the two new laureates returned home with the wrong medals. An easily resolved problem. Except that Leonid Kantorovich was a Russian and Tjalling Koopmans was an American. In a process that matched the delicate negotiations for political prisoner exchanges, it took years of diplomatic efforts to exchange the medals.

Burglars and Bunglers

If you are going to steal a Nobel Prize medal, it might be wise to (1) lay low for a while and (2) not impersonate a police officer. Had Russ (we'll use just his first name) done so, the Salt Lake City resident could have saved himself a lot of trouble. In January 2007, Russ was arrested for impersonating a police officer, a misdemeanor in Utah. The man who turned Russ in also had a criminal record and needed to report to his own probation officer. Without his own transportation, the man asked Russ's girlfriend to drive him to Utah Probation and Parole so he would make it there on time. The girlfriend not only agreed to act as chauffer but used Russ's car, which was available since Russ was sitting in jail. After reaching the parole office, and for reasons unknown, the two opened the trunk and found a gun. The police were notified and did a thorough search of the trunk. Among the items discovered was a Nobel Peace Prize medal belonging to Kay Miller, the 1985 recipient. The thief had lived in the basement of Miller's home the prior fall. The good news was that the medal had been found. The bad news was that Russ had disappeared. His mother had paid his lower misdemeanor bail before the police could add felony charges, and Russell was in the wind.

Another rule you should avoid is showing off things that you steal, especially something as unique as a Nobel Prize medal. In 2007, the 1939 Nobel Prize medal awarded to physicist Ernest Lawrence was stolen from a display case at the University of California, Berkeley, Lawrence Hall of Science. A work-study student had the sudden urge to remove the medal from its locked display case. Within a few days, he was showing it off to friends, which ultimately led to his arrest. To his credit, the student had stored the medal in a safe place – the attic of his parents' home an hour away.

Apparently, stealing works best if you pick a day when there will be distractions. In 2004, author Rabindranath Tagore's 1913 Nobel Prize medal was stolen from a museum at Visva Bharati University. The medal was among dozens of items stolen from specific storage areas that the thieves must have been confident they had time to open. That was the day of the India vs. Pakistan cricket match. Sources said that security personnel were watching the event on television.

As any competent burglar knows, you should avoid leaving clues to your identity. In 2010, Roy Glauber, the 2005 Nobel laureate in physics, returned home to find that his house had been ransacked during his absence. Among the missing items was his gold medal. Normally, solving home burglaries has a poor success rate – unless the perpetrator leaves a clue. Or two. Or three. Or four. In a spare bedroom police found a used cigarette on the nightstand as well as a hair follicle on a pillow. Inside the broken window used to gain entry, police observed a Hannaford Supermarket bag of half-eaten food. Elsewhere there was a container of smoked oysters and a receipt showing the date of the transaction. The thief had used a food stamp card to make the purchase. Food stamps are traceable. Authorities obtained video of the supermarket register for the time in question, which confirmed the identity of the person as the owner of the food stamp card. When asked by the Boston Herald to comment on the investigation, the Arlington, Massachusetts, police chief noted that the victim and the alleged perpetrator were on opposite ends of the IQ spectrum.

In one case, the recovery of a stolen Nobel medal involved some unlikely allies – the Castro family of Cuba. Ernest Hemingway spent many winters in Cuba, writing famous novels such as *The Old Man and the Sea*. He appreciated the Cuban people so much that he donated his 1954 Nobel Prize gold medal to the people of Cuba (an important distinction for the country of Cuba). Hemingway placed the medal under the care of the Catholic Church to be displayed in El Cobre, a small town on the island's southeast coast. In 1986, thieves broke into the sanctuary and snatched the medal. One might think that a medal stolen from a rural Cuban church would not be a priority to the Cuban government. The Castro family, however, considered Hemingway a national treasure and were determined to solve the mystery. Raul Castro, now vice president, purportedly published an official ultimatum stating, "Return the medal within 72 hours or face the consequences. I know who you are." Shortly afterward, the missing medal miraculously reappeared at the church.

So, Why Were You in Fargo?

Sometimes Nobel winners can be too smart for their own good. Brian Schmidt, winner of the 2011 Nobel Prize in Physics, learned this the hard way, as he tried to convince airport security that a $10,000 gold medal that he was bringing home to Australia was really his. As Schmidt described to an audience in 2014, even Nobel Prize winners were not immune from travel hassles.

> When I won this [referring to the big, thick, half-pound gold disk], my grandma, who lives in Fargo, North Dakota, wanted to see it. I was coming around, so I decided I'd bring my Nobel Prize. You would think that carrying around a Nobel Prize would be uneventful, and it was uneventful, until I tried to leave Fargo with it and went through the X-ray machine. I could see they were puzzled. It was in my laptop bag. It's made of gold, so it absorbs all the X-rays — it's completely black. And they had never seen anything completely black.
>
> They're like, "Sir, there's something in your bag."
>
> I said, "Yes, I think it's this box."
>
> They said, "What's in the box?"
>
> I said, "A large gold medal," as one does.
>
> So they opened it up and they said, "What's it made out of?"
>
> I said, "Gold."
>
> And they're like, "Uhhhh. Who gave this to you?"
>
> "The King of Sweden."
>
> "Why did he give this to you?"
>
> "Because I helped discover the expansion rate of the universe was accelerating."
>
> At which point, they were beginning to lose their sense of humor. I explained to them it was a Nobel Prize, and their main question was, "Why were you in Fargo?"

Going Once, Going Twice, Sold!

Nobel Prize medals have been auctioned for a variety of reasons and for sums that have ranged from the paltry to the astronomical. Aristide Briand's 1926 Peace Prize medal holds the distinction as the lowest priced medal ($14,000 in 2008). Briand's medal also holds the distinction of being the only medal to be both auctioned and stolen. Purchased in 2008 by Heritage

Museum Écomusée of Saint-Nazaire, France, the medal was subsequently stolen in 2015 and remains missing.

On the opposite end of the scale, Dmitry Muratov's 2021 Nobel Peace Prize medal sold at auction for a record $103.5 million in 2022. This auction was notable for several reasons. First, Muratov was a living Nobel laureate. Second, Muratov received no personal gain whatsoever from the sale. Last, the auction took place on June 20, coinciding with the annual date for World Refugee Day. Kudos to Dmitry Muratov for being such a noble Nobel laureate.

James Watson, another living Nobel laureate, auctioned his medal in 2014, but his story is much different and not nearly so noble. Watson is best known for his work on the structure of DNA, which earned him a share of the 1962 Nobel Prize in Physiology or Medicine. His reputation, however, became tarnished after he commented publicly in 2007 that Black people were not as intelligent as Whites. Watson lost his appointment as chancellor at New York's Cold Spring Harbor Laboratory. Speaking invitations and grant support also disappeared. He further harmed his standing in the scientific community when he reinforced his belief in a Public Broadcasting Corporation documentary. Ostracized for the most part, Watson decided to auction his Nobel medal, which netted over $4 million. He also became one of the luckiest Nobel laureates ever when the purchaser of the medal, a Russian billionaire, gifted the medal back to Watson. Which introduces a taxing topic for budding accountants to ponder. How much did Watson have to pay in taxes from the proceeds of his auctioned medal? If his medal was gifted back to him, must Watson pay taxes on its value (what it once sold for)? If it ever comes to that, Watson always has one option. He can auction it once again.

Leon Lederman was the third living laureate to auction a Nobel medal. He shared the 1988 Nobel Prize in Physics, but even a Nobel Prize could not save a famous person from old age, rising health care costs, and depleted savings. In 2011, the eighty-nine-year-old Lederman began experiencing memory loss, which progressed to severe dementia. Medicare did not cover the necessary costs needed for such patients. Lederman was forced to sell his Nobel medal in 2015 to help pay for his medical expenses and nursing home care. He died in an Idaho nursing home in 2018. Lederman, an atheist, was known as the father of "the God particle." Whether its citizens be atheist, Jew, or Christian, what would God think about a country where a person needs to sell personal possessions to pay for medical care? Perhaps politicians know. Perhaps they don't care.

Carlos Saavedra Lamas's gold medal sold at auction in 2014 for $1.16 million, far above the expected price of $50,000 anticipated by a New York auction house. But the unusual price paid for the medal once owned by the 1936 Peace Prize winner might be the least unusual part of the story. Lamas died in 1959, so he was not the current owner of the auctioned gold medal. Nor did his relatives or estate initiate the sale, which has been the more traditional route for an auctioned Nobel medal. The story of Lamas's medal is the sort of thing one would see on *The Antiques Roadshow*, where a $5 purchase at a garage sale is valued at $500,000. At the 2014 auction, Lamas's gold medal was sold to an Asian bidder who wished to remain anonymous. The seller was the estate of a coin expert who had acquired the medal when he purchased the Charles Warton Collection years earlier. The coin collector had procured it from someone, who had procured it from someone else, who had found it in an unknown pawn shop while traveling in South America –the owner of which had acquired it from yet another person back in 1993. The pawn shop paid only the value of the gold, which would have been about $3,100 at that time (roughly $10,000 today). Sensing that the medal might be worth more as a curiosity to a collector, the pawnshop owner decided to hang onto it for a while rather than dumping it into the bin of rings and earrings that were typically melted down and sold as bullion. Even if Carlos Lamas had his Nobel medal in his possession at the time of his death in 1959, where the gold medal resided for the next thirty-four years is still unknown.

Hidden in Plain Sight

Georgy de Hevesy breathed a sigh of relief. He could not believe that he had accomplished his mission before the soldiers came. Had they found it, there would have been swift justice. It was there, sitting on the shelf, but the soldiers passed it by. Don't move it. Just leave it as it is and recover it another day. What the soldiers were looking for was gold. Gold to fund the Third Reich during World War II. Gold, the only currency that cooperating countries would accept from Germany.

When Adolf Hitler rose to power in the 1930s, he began appropriating much of the gold in Germany from citizens and businesses. To Hitler, gold was a symbol of wealth or accomplishment. It represented the individual over the Motherland. Gold should not be owned but rather given to the government for the benefit of the people. By dictum, no gold should leave Germany. This did not deter many German citizens from sending gold outside of the country. Two German Nobel Prize in Physics winners, Max von Laue (1914) and James Franck (1925), sent their 23-carat gold medals to colleague and 1922 physics laureate Niels Bohr, who ran the Institute of Theoretical Physics in Copenhagen. The gold medals should have been safe there.

In 1940, however, the Nazis captured Copenhagen. Soldiers searched homes and buildings for any usable materials, especially gold. Niels Bohr also had a Nobel medal, but he had donated it to be auctioned earlier that year to raise money for Finnish Relief. But he still had in his possession von Laue's and Franck's gold medals, each showing the name of the person who owned it. Niels Bohr faced punishment for simply having the gold, and the two German Nobel laureates faced punishment for not just owning but also shipping gold outside of the country. The contraband needed to be hidden.

Bohr called one of his laboratory assistants, Georgy de Hevesy, asking him to do something. Quickly. If the time pressure was not enough, de Hevesy faced the challenge of hiding the two pieces of shiny metal that each weighed nearly a half a pound. He couldn't just wave his hand and change the gold into tin. He couldn't paint the gold, bury it, or hide it behind a wall or under a floorboard. Nazi soldiers knew all the tricks and, if necessary, would tear a property apart.

Fortunately, de Hevesy was a chemist rather than a physicist like his colleague Bohr. He wondered if it might be possible to dissolve the medals. But how? Gold was one of the noble metals, which were remarkably stable, not oxidizable, resistant to even the smallest amount of corrosion, and not dissolvable in solvents. Think, think, think! The answer came to him. de Hevesy recalled the liquid aqua regia (Latin for royal water) that was developed around the year 800, in which one part nitric acid was combined with three parts hydrochloric acid, creating a reagent that could dissolve metals such as gold. Individually, each acid did little, but the two combined worked wonders. The final product, chloroaurate, created a yellow-orange–looking solution. de Hevesy placed the flask holding the gold/aqua regia on a shelf that held dozens of other flasks. It looked like any other flask holding one of the many chemicals used in the laboratory. But hidden in plain sight.

In 1943, de Hevesy, himself a Jewish scientist, was forced to escape Denmark for his own safety, landing in Sweden. He spent the rest of his career at Stockholm University. Max von Laue's and James Franck's medals, however, were not lost to history. After the war ended, de Hevesy went back to visit his old laboratory and discovered the yellow-orange solution still sitting on the shelf. He performed a reverse chemical reaction, recovered the gold, and returned it to the Swedish Academy of Sciences. The Nobel Foundation had the gold medals recast and presented a second time to their rightful owners.

Niels Bohr's gold medal never ended up back in his possession. Bohr, however, retained one enduring benefit of having received the Nobel Prize. In 1932, the Carlsberg Corporation donated a house adjacent to the brewery for Bohr and his family to live in. The house also came with free beer. Niels Bohr took advantage of both for the next thirty years.

CHAPTER SIX

A Medal for Mickey Mouse

Marjorie, Martina, Milton. Their contributions were critical to the discovery of insulin, the field of ethology, and our concepts of physics. Because of them, others received Nobel Prizes. Yet, you won't find their names listed next to the Nobel laureates who worked with them. That's because Marjorie was a dog. Martina was a goose. And Milton was a cat.

Animals have played an important role in Nobel Prizes as far back as 1901, the first year the awards were presented. Most of the discoveries that have led to the Nobel Prize in Physiology or Medicine have come about because of animal research. The contributions of animals, however, have gone beyond medicine to include Nobel Prizes in Literature, Physics, Economics, and Peace.

Mice

The word *rodent* usually evokes a negative response from people. Billions of mice, however, have given their lives for the betterment of humankind. Because mice have been less a source of inspiration and more a tool to achieve a goal, mice have received little if any respect, with one exception: a mouse originally named Mortimer. Mortimer is the only animal to be successfully nominated for a Nobel Prize. Two young men created a fictitious peace institute and then used it to nominate a mouse for the Nobel Peace Prize. Surprisingly, the nomination was accepted but did not receive serious consideration. The Nobel Foundation does not award prizes to animals – not even the world's most famous mouse. Walt Disney's mouse is not known by his original name, Mortimer, but rather the name that Walt's wife Lillian preferred: Mickey. Yes, Mickey Mouse was nominated for a Nobel Prize in 2020.

Insects

The first Nobel Prize associated with insects was awarded in 1902 to British physician Ronald Ross. Growing up in India, Ross wanted more than anything to be a poet. His father, a general, thought otherwise and convinced his son to go into medicine. Ronald eventually ended up back in India, where his research earned him the Nobel Prize in Physiology or Medicine for his discovery that mosquitos transmitted the parasite that caused malaria. He allowed mosquitos to suck blood from malaria-infected people and, after tedious dissection of the mosquitos, found the malaria parasite at a certain stage of life in the stomachs of the mosquitos.

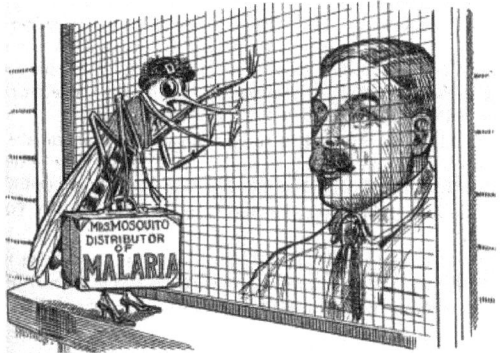

Ronald Ross vs. Mrs. Mosquito. From 1922 Virginia Health Bulletin. Courtesy of Virginia Commonwealth University Libraries, Special Collections and Archives.

Ross had shown, for the first time, the principle of vector-borne disease. What did Ross do after his discovery? He wrote a poem about it. One that you might recognize, although you would never guess it was an ode to a mosquito:

> This day relenting God
> Hath placed within my hand
> A wondrous thing; and God
> Be praised. At His command,
> Seeking His secret deeds
> With tears and toiling breath,
> I find thy cunning seeds,
> O million-murdering Death.
> I know this little thing
> A myriad men will save.
> O Death, where is thy sting?
> Thy victory, O Grave?

§

If you hate mosquitos, consider lice. In 1928, Charles Jules Henri Nicolle won the Nobel Prize in Physiology or Medicine for his work on body lice and typhus. Nicolle was a bacteriologist whose most important discovery did not emerge from a laboratory but rather a serendipitous field observation.

Typhus was recognized as a terrible and lethal disease, but little was known about how it was transmitted and therefore how to control it. In 1903, when Charles Nicolle arrived in Tunis to head the Pasteur Institute, he noted the seasonality of typhus outbreaks, especially in rural areas. The winter months saw an explosion of cases and deaths, which disappeared during the summer. Rural prisons were especially hard hit. It was while visiting one prison that Nicolle had his Aha! moment. He observed that of the personnel who came into initial contact with typhus patients, such as admissions staff, laundry workers who delivered hospital gowns and gathered patient clothing, and admitting physicians, nearly all caught the disease. But none of the doctors or nurses who treated these same sick patients in the general wards became infected; sick patients but no transmission to staff. Most unusual. But that breakthrough observation set the foundation for future work. As Nicolle stated in his 1929 Nobel lecture: "I took this observation as my guide. I asked myself what happened between the entrance to the hospital and the wards. This is what happened: the typhus patient was stripped of his clothes and linen, shaved and washed. The contagious agent was therefore something attached to his skin and clothing, something which soap and water could remove. It could only be the louse. It was the louse."

Did Charles Nicolle ever catch typhus himself? No. His observation that nonsanitary practices increased the chances of infection and death was a factor. But an earlier episode that saved his life was even more important. Nicolle had asked to accompany a doctor who was treating scores of prisoners with typhus. The day before the visit, Nicolle coughed up some blood and was forced to bow out. A colleague of his, Dr. René Motheau, and a servant, went ahead with the visit, arriving the night before and staying on the premises. Both contracted typhus and died. If not for serendipity, Charles Nicolle's first encounter with typhus would have been his last.

§

Ants in a bathroom would cause most people to reach for the bug spray. But not 1965 Nobel laureate Richard Feynman, who walked into his bathroom one day and noticed ants emerging from a hole and wandering around his bathtub. As described in his book, *Surely You're Joking, Mr. Feynman*, he considered this an opportunity to observe their behavior. Feynman placed some sugar at the far end of the bathtub and waited. And waited. And waited. An ant finally discovered the sugar. Feynman grabbed a colored pencil and drew a line that followed the trail the ant created on its way back to the hole. The ant wandered away from the clear path to the hole, creating a wiggly line. When a second ant found its way to the sugar and then began returning to the hole, Feynman followed its path using a different colored pencil. The second ant, sensing a trail left by the first ant, moved much more quickly, sometimes "coasting" in a straight path until it found the trail again (imagine a windy road in the mountains where engineers finally decide that it is more efficient to cut a tunnel through one mountain rather than take a long road around the mountain). The second ant ended up taking a somewhat straighter journey. Each successive ant "coasted" its way to a straighter path than the ones before it. By the time ten ants had returned home, the path had become a straight line. The ants had unknowingly played a part in Feynman's theories about quantum electrodynamics, in which he studied how particles influence one another as they move between two points. In this case, ants moving between sugar and home. To Feynman, the sum image of the ants' paths had a similarity to a composite of the diagrams that Feynman had proposed to explain particle interactions. It's been said that a seemingly simple decision made in the present can greatly influence the future. Richard Feynman's decision is proof of this. Rather than reaching for bug spray, Feynman reached for sugar. And won a Nobel Prize.

§

Of all the insects that have contributed to a Nobel Prize, the unassuming fruit fly is the champion. *Drosophila melanogaster* – the common fruit fly – has been the model organism for six Nobel Prizes. Thomas Hunt Morgan, winner of the 1933 Nobel Prize in Physiology or Medicine, used fruit flies in his work on the chromosomal theory of inheritance. Morgan had a "fly room" in his laboratory where he kept a supply of ripe bananas for his fruit fly subjects. The fruit flies were housed in glass milk bottles that his students stole from apartment steps.

Hermann Muller, recipient of the 1946 Nobel Prize in Physiology or Medicine, also studied fruit flies and showed the link between radiation exposure and genetic mutations. By the time he received the award, Muller had become vocal about unnecessary exposures to radiation and the resulting risks of genetic abnormalities and cancer. The Atomic Energy Commission, one of his targets, deemed him a nuisance and refused to let him present a paper in Geneva on the hazards of radiation at the United Nations International Conference on the Peaceful Use of Atomic Energy.

Morgan's fly room at Columbia University. Public domain.
PD-US.

Undeterred, Muller registered as a general attendee. Muller never said a word. He did not need to. Nearly every presenter referenced his work. Muller received a standing ovation.

Hermann Muller (right) using a jeweler's loupe to see his tiny subjects. Courtesy Lilly Library, Indiana University, Bloomington, Indiana.

A half-century later, three researchers from different institutions shared the 1995 Nobel Prize in Physiology or Medicine for demonstrating how embryonic cells, all of which start out appearing identical, change and then begin to create individual parts of the body such as the eyes, heart, and legs. Working with fruit flies, Edward Lewis, Christiane Nüsslein-Volhard, and Eric Wieschaus demonstrated that genes were arranged on a chromosome in the same positions as the final body layout (genes for the head, followed by genes for the abdomen, followed by genes for the rear portion). The next time someone questions whether your head is on straight or suggests that it might be located elsewhere, you can state that your head is exactly where it should be, and fruit flies will back you up.

Fruit flies have also helped us answer why the smell of baked bread helps sell a house. Or why one perfume or cologne elicits attraction while another has the opposite effect. Or how we smell at all. Richard Axel and Linda Buck, who shared the 2004 Nobel Prize in Physiology or Medicine, identified the neural coding for olfactory sensory stimuli in fruit fly brains. Compounds in the air reach specialized nerve cells, where they bind like a key into a lock. This lock-and-key complex sets off signals that the brain perceives as smell. Interestingly, the specialized nerve cells are located on their antennae and mouth, in contrast to humans, whose nerve cells are in the nose.

In 2017, researchers Jeffrey Hall, Michael Rosbash, and Michael Young shared the Nobel Prize in Physiology or Medicine for their discoveries of the molecular mechanisms driving circadian rhythms, the internal clocks that synchronize biology and behavior to the day-night cycle. Their work revealed that the genes that drive sleep (and the mutations that alter sleep) in humans parallel those found in fruit flies. Another fact for your next trivia competition: just like humans, caffeine keeps fruit flies awake. In fact, caffeine supplements have been shown to produce increased sex drive in male fruit flies. The next time you find a fly in your coffee, he might be getting ready for a date.

§

Perhaps the most beautiful insect is the butterfly. Butterflies were special to Gabriel García Márquez, recipient of the 1982 Nobel Prize in Literature. His home country, Colombia, had thousands of butterfly species. The favored colors of this country – vibrant yellows, blues, greens, and reds often seen on painted buildings and in dyed cotton clothing – reflect the colors of these winged beauties. Marquez especially loved yellow butterflies and gave them a prominent place in his best-known novel, *One Hundred Years of Solitude*. The book and its author were so treasured by the people of Colombia that yellow butterflies became a national symbol of the country. At the many memorials following Márquez's death at age eighty-seven, people carried yellow paper butterflies.

Butterflies have also played an essential role in the Nobel Peace Prize.

Scientist Camille Parmesan discovered that butterflies were a better measure of temperature change than a thermometer. Studying location changes of the temperature-sensitive Edith's checkerspot butterfly, Parmesan observed that the butterflies had moved to higher latitudes as well as higher elevations after experiencing a 0.7-degree centigrade temperature increase over the study period, proof that climate change affected living creatures. Recognition of the importance of her work led to Parmesan's appointment as a lead author for the Intergovernmental Panel on Climate Change, which shared the 2007 Nobel Peace Prize with Al Gore.

Camille Parmesan with mating pairs of checkerspot butterflies on her fingers. Photograph by and courtesy of Michael C. Singer, University of Plymouth.

§

Karl von Frisch was famous for his descriptions of the individual and social behavior patterns of bees. Recipient of the 1973 Nobel Prize in Physiology or Medicine, von Frisch demonstrated the importance of what would be considered "language" in bees. When a bee discovers an external source of honey, it returns to the hive and performs a dance. The type of dance depends on the distance of the honey source from the hive. The dance takes place inside the dark hive, with straight-line and turning movements telling fellow bees the direction and distance from the hive to the source, rather like nature's GPS.

Even when it is dark outside, bees can tell direction via polarized, ultraviolet light as well as magnetic fields. In his 1927 book, *Aus dem Leben der Bienen* (The Dancing Bees), von Frisch wrote about the behavior of bees. This book has been described as a model example of how simple science can be performed without sophisticated instruments. Beekeepers refer to this book as a guide to understanding bees. Yet, scientists still take sides when it comes to his observations and resulting conclusions. His work continues to create a buzz.

Figure-eight-shaped waggle dance of the honeybee. A waggle run (wavy line) oriented 45° to the right indicates a food source 45° to the right of the direction of the sun outside the hive. (Lars Chittka, "Dances as Windows into Insect Perception," *PLoS Biology* 2, no. 7 [2014]: e216. https://doi.org/10.1371/journal.pbio.0020216)

§

Insects have even contributed to the field of economics. And nothing says Nobel Prize quite like a fly in a urinal. Just ask Richard Thaler, winner of the 2017 Nobel Prize in Economics. Thaler, an expert in behavioral economics, developed a theory based on the idea that people do not make choices in isolation. People need structure (a.k.a. choice architecture) to make decisions. The key is to develop structures that help people make better decisions or lead individuals towards a desired decision. Sometimes people need to be *nudged* in a certain direction. Richard Thaler and coauthor Cass Sunstein introduced nudge theory in their 2009 book *Nudge: Improving Decisions about Health, Wealth, and Happiness*. Thaler and Sunstein consider a nudge as any intervention "that alters people's behavior in a predictable way without forbidding any options or significantly changing their economic incentives." The key to a nudge is that it must not act like a command or rule. In fact, a nudge should not require an individual to do anything. A nudge does not forbid doing the wrong thing but rather makes it easier to do the right thing. Great in principle, but where is the proof? Well, it exists. Thaler and Sunstein provide an example so fundamental to proving nudge theory that it appears within the first four pages of their book. It is the fly in a urinal.

Fly sticker in urinal. Author creation.

Some thirty years ago, a manager at Amsterdam's Schiphol Airport noted the constant dirtiness of the men's bathrooms, especially spillage around the urinals. There were cleaning personnel, but by the time they completed one round, the floors were dirty again. The problem was simple. Men didn't aim. There was no incentive. The manager could not prevent men from being careless, but perhaps he could subtly nudge them in a desired direction. So, the manager had a fly etched onto the inside of the urinal, which provided the user with a target. It worked like a charm. Without being told what to do, men did exactly what the manager wanted. Aim at the fly. Spillage went down by 80 percent. Bathrooms needed less frequent cleaning. No customer was ordered to do anything. Customers could have peed wherever they wanted. Yet, they did the proper thing because they were nudged in a certain direction.

There is also both a *why* and *where* component to the solution. Why a fly? Spiders are considered creepy, and customers might avoid that urinal. Bees are easy to see, but if you miss them, they might chase after you. Flies, however, are associated with unkempt surroundings. People have few reservations about aiming at them. But, where to place the fly? In many places the fly is situated just above the drain and to the left. Why? Because more men are right-handed. Ask a right-handed male to grasp a carrot and see where it points. Makes sense now. Since that original lightbulb moment in Amsterdam, fake flies have appeared in bathrooms around the globe. There are companies that manufacturer peel-and-stick flies. There are even flies that glow in the dark.

Having come up with a solution to why men don't aim – or even try to aim – the next nudge breakthrough will hopefully solve the age-old problem of how to get men to lower the toilet seat. I once listened as a man described an encounter where his significant other marched him into the bathroom and asked why he never put the toilet seat back where it belonged. He responded, "Because I don't want to." That's what's called a wrong answer.

Birds

In 1909, Peyton Rous opened the door to his Rockefeller Institute laboratory and found himself face-to-face with a Barred Plymouth Rock chicken. Holding the bird was a local farmer who had noticed an egg-sized lump on the chicken's breast. Pathologists studied lumps, and Rous was a pathologist.

Chicken with Peyton Rous's tumor. Used with permission of Rockefeller University Press from P. Rous, "A Transmissible Avian Neoplasm, Sarcoma of the Common Fowl," *J. Exp. Med.* 12, no. 5 (1910). Permission conveyed through Copyright Clearance Center, Inc.

A biopsy of the lump showed it to be a sarcoma, an unusual malignant tumor that affected the connective tissue. Rous wondered whether the tumor would spread among the other chickens at the farm – whether it was contagious. Rous ground up a piece of the tumor, filtered the mixture to remove the cells and other structural elements of the breast muscle, and injected the fluid into other Barred Plymouth Rock chickens. The chickens developed tumors, which became more aggressive with each passage of tumor filtrates. Some ultrasmall organism, likely a virus, was the culprit behind the cancers. Rous published his observations and transmission theory in 1911.

None of the experts in the field of oncology believed that a virus could cause cancer. No one thought that his ideas were worth verifying. It took another fifty years for science to catch up and properly recognize the now-famous Rous sarcoma virus. Peyton Rous finally got his due when he was awarded the Nobel Prize in Physiology or Medicine in 1966. He was 87 years old at that time, no spring chicken. While Rous was receiving the Nobel Prize, two scientists in their thirties, Harold Varmus and Michael Bishop, were just ramping up experiments in oncology focused on studying viral gene mutations and cancer. Varmus and Bishop later received the Nobel Prize for their discoveries. What virus did they study? Peyton Rous's virus. What animal model did they use? The chicken.

Today, if you asked someone to define beriberi, chances are that they would think it was a fruit drink. Beriberi, however, is a progressive disease that starts with overall body weakness, followed by burning sensation of the limbs, followed by paralysis that makes it difficult to walk. Yet, it is a disease with a simple cure, requiring only an improved diet that includes the proper vitamins.

One hundred years ago, we had little idea that vitamins even existed and were essential to living organisms. The great discovery of vitamins came about because of the intersection of two unlikely things: war and chickens. Christiaan Eijkman encountered both and, through a set of interesting circumstances, walked away with a share of the 1929 Nobel Prize in Physiology or Medicine for the discovery of thiamine (vitamin B). During the Dutch colonial period, the country was involved in a military conflict with Indonesia. The Dutch military leadership noted that soldiers sent to the war zone became debilitated after a few weeks and showed signs of beriberi. The Dutch government created a commission that included Eijkman to determine what was causing the beriberi. Sensing that there might be a pathogen responsible, Eijkman injected chickens that were being kept at the outpost with blood from soldiers who had the disease and compared the results to chickens that had not been injected. Every chicken from both groups got sick. Beriberi was not caused by an infectious agent. Eijkman brought in more chickens and made sure that the new flock was well isolated from any diseased animals. The new chickens got sick. But then they suddenly got well! Same chickens, same chicken coop. Dying, then thriving. Eijkman thought that perhaps the chickens had temporarily been given some contaminated feed that later had been replaced with a fresh shipment. Talking to the worker in charge of feeding the animals, Eijkman learned that, to save money, this individual had been feeding the chickens polished, cooked white rice that was left over from a nearby hospital. The cook at the hospital had learned of this and put a stop to feeding chickens high-quality polished rice that was meant for people. The chickens went back to receiving uncooked, unpolished rice on nearly the same date that the chickens started getting back to normal. Aha! The brown husk on rice contained some compound that was essential for avoiding beriberi. The essential nutritional element was eventually identified as vitamin B. During the next decade, other vitamins were identified, including vitamins A, E, and C. It took a war, a flock of chickens, and a clever scientist to solve the mystery.

§

Martina was instrumental to Konrad Lorenz's career. The two were inseparable. She shared his bed, comforted him when he was down, even contributed to his ideas on imprinting in animals. Then, one day, she found another male and was gone for good. To be fair, Martina was better off with her new partner Martin, who had more in common with Martina than did Konrad Lorenz. Because Martina and Martin were geese.

Lorenz admitted that, when he was a boy, he yearned to become a wild goose. Knowing that this was not possible, Lorenz wanted to have one. This was realized in 1935 when Martina the graylag goose hatched from an egg inside the Lorenz home. She imprinted (i.e., formed an attachment) on the first object she saw, which was Konrad Lorenz. Lorenz saw this as something magically innate to many animals and became Martina's foster mother as the goose grew and ultimately left home.

That same year, Lorenz performed his best-known imprinting experiment. He divided a group of graylag goose eggs that were just about to hatch into two groups. One group of eggs was placed under a female goose. The goslings immediately followed the mother. Group two was hatched in an incubator. These goslings saw Lorenz as the first mother figure and followed him. In a subsequent experiment, Lorenz combined the two groups of goslings into one large box, from which they could not see the goose mother or Lorenz, and let them mix for a while. After releasing them, each group immediately went to their original mothers, be it Lorenz or the real goose. Imprinting (attachment) was clearly a permanent effect, not a temporary one that lasted just a few days.

Konrad Lorenz with Martina. Courtesy of Riccardo Draghi-Lorenz.

Lorenz continued throughout his career to study the social behavior of animals, for which he won the 1973 Nobel Prize in Physiology or Medicine. Lorenz became equally famous for his many books on animal behavior and its relevance to human behavior. The same year that Martina and Martin left on their new adventures, Martina appeared in an essay by Lorenz as a character called "Ma." Lorenz continued to include Martina in his books, from *King Solomon's Ring* to his final book in 1988, *Here I Am – Where Are You?* Very few animals, let alone humans, have attained fame in both the scientific and general literature. A honking good achievement.

§

National Pigeon Appreciation Day is celebrated each year on June 13. Yes, there is such a day, started by President Woodrow Wilson shortly after the end of World War 1 to recognize the 150,000 pigeons that delivered critical messages from the battlefield. June 13 was specifically selected to honor Cher Ami, a pigeon that saved 194 soldiers who were being accidently bombed by their own artillery brigade. Since this is a book about Nobel

Prizes, however, let's celebrate the contributions of pigeons to the Nobel Prizes before returning to Cher Ami.

During the early part of the twentieth century, scientists were trying to determine how animals converted food into energy to power their cells. To do that, a suitable model was needed that could rapidly and consistently produce energy under experimental conditions. Pigeons fit the bill for two reasons. First, pigeons were strong flyers, able to fly for long distances at a fast pace. Pigeon breast muscles (pectoralis major), the chief flight muscles capable of lifting more than ten times the bird's weight, and which represented a large percentage of the total weight of a single bird, proved to be the ideal organ for metabolic energy studies. Second, there was a cheap supply of pigeons. Albert Szent-Györgyi and Hans Krebs, recipients of the 1937 and 1953 Nobel Prize in Physiology or Medicine, respectively, perfected the use of pigeon breast muscle slices and homogenates to identify two of the most important metabolic pathways for converting food energy into energy that powers the body.

§

Whenever you have pigeons, you likely have something else: pigeon poop. And it is pigeon poop that played a role in confirming the existence of the big bang (not the television show) origin of the universe. In 1960, Bell Laboratories constructed a megaphone-shaped antenna in Holmdel, New Jersey, that was fifty feet in length and twenty feet wide at the opening. Initially intended as a radio signal relay device, the antenna soon fell out of use because of new satellites.

Two Bell employees asked if they could use the now defunct antenna to map signals from the Milky Way. Fine with Bell Laboratories. So, in 1964, Arno Penzias and Robert Wilson began collecting radio waves from outer space. When the two scientists turned on the antenna, they encountered a weird microwave noise that persisted regardless of the antenna's direction.

Penzias and Wilson fixed dings in the sheet metal and taped rough edges around the funnel. The hum was still there. Having exhausted all engineering options, they finally looked deep into the funnel and saw two pigeons living there, along with all the poop that covered the walls. The scientists captured the pigeons with a Havahart cage trap and took them thirty miles away. Mission accomplished, or so they thought. The antenna and funnel were thoroughly cleaned, and new readings begun.

The Holmdel horn antenna. NASA, public domain. PD-USGov-NASA.

Within two days, however, the two pigeons had found their way home, and the poop challenge began anew. With the help of a hunting friend, the two pigeons were permanently dispatched, the antenna cleaned once more, and the radio signals measured again. Surprise! If anything, the background noise was even greater than when the pigeons were around. Future experiments confirmed that what the duo had discovered was cosmic microwave background radiation resulting from the big bang billions of years ago. Penzias and Wilson shared the 1978 Nobel Prize in Physics. Since that time, the Holmdel Antenna has been designated a National Historic Landmark. The metal cage used to trap the pigeons now resides at the National Air and Space Museum in Washington, DC. Across the street, at the National Museum of American History, you can visit Cher Ami, the most famous pigeon of all. Cher Ami is on display next to Sergeant Stubby, the part Boston Terrier mascot of the Army's 102nd Infantry.

Cats

Economics laureates George Akerlof (in 2001), and Robert Shiller (in 2013), gained international recognition for their work on how human emotions play a role in economic decision making. Anyone who remembers Alan Greenspan's warning about "irrational exuberance" in the 1990s, prior to the dot-com collapse, knows how human emotions and expectations can exceed reality. Akerlof and Shiller wrote a book titled *Phishing for Phools*, in which they studied how companies profit by tempting people to make decisions that are good for the company but bad for the customer. As part of their research, they decided to test an everyday type of purchase: cat food.

Robert Shiller had a cat named Lightning, and Shiller spared no expense in giving his feline friend the best. Cat food cans not only had colorful images of happy, satisfied cats on the labels, but also descriptions that sounded like a menu at a fine restaurant. Perhaps something irresistible like "Roasted Chicken Delight Plus Giblet Gravy." The cat food must taste like the label indicated if the company said so. To find out the truth, Shiller tasted various canned cat foods. Yes, a Nobel laureate consumed cat food in the name of economic science. His conclusion? They all had a similar taste. They tasted like cat food.

In the interest of conducting a proper crossover experiment, perhaps Robert Shiller should have taken some expensive wines from his collection – the ones with overtones of stone fruit, exceptional nose, artistic labels, and high Wine Spectator scores – and let Lightning taste them. Wouldn't it be ironic if they all tasted the same to the cat? If they tasted like wine?

§

In the 1930s, future physics prize recipient Erwin Schrödinger was living in Oxford, England, with his wife, his mistress, and a cat named Milton. When not dividing his attention between the two women, the quantum physicist developed a novel equation that could predict the behavior of subatomic particles. At this tiny scale, subatomic particles behaved differently than what might be observed in the larger world. So, Schrödinger put things in terms of probabilities (A or B). Disagreeing with Schrödinger's probability theory, some physicists argued that it might be possible for two incompatible states (both A and B) to coexist until some event caused a shift from one state to another (A or B). Schrödinger believed that this hypothesis was impossible and developed a thought experiment to point out the absurdity of his colleagues' logic. The experiment involved a cat (i.e., Milton) being placed in a sealed box containing a weak radioactive material, a Geiger counter, a vial of cyanide, and a hammer trip mechanism. A clock was then set for one hour. If during that time the radioactive substance decayed and emitted a particle of radiation, the Geiger counter would detect it, triggering the hammer to fall and break the cyanide vial, which would kill the cat. During the one hour wait, maybe the radioactive substance did emit a particle, and the cat might be dead. But, being a weak radioactive substance, it's just as likely that it did not decay and therefore the cat could be alive.

Filming Schrödinger's cat. Until the film is developed,
the cat could be alive or dead. Wikipedia Commons,
Christian Schirm. CC0 1.0.

Since the box was sealed, however, no one could observe what happened,
so the cat was in an unknowable state. It was both dead and alive (A and B).
It was not until the box was opened that the answer would be clear whether
the cat was alive or dead (A or B). Everyone agreed that this was crazy. A
cat could not be simultaneously alive and dead. To which Erwin Schrödinger
said thank you. A cat had proven him right.

§

Sometimes you can eat cat food to test an idea. Sometimes you can use
an imaginary cat. But sometimes it becomes necessary to perform
experiments directly on animals. In the 1960s, surgical treatment for
congenital cataracts (clouding of the eye in infants) was postponed until
patients reached an age where the eyes were larger and more developed.
Although there was general success, many patients still had impaired vision
that failed to fully resolve. What would cause a usually successful surgical
operation to be followed by variable outcomes? Was there some
unidentified early visual developmental process that was crucial to full
eyesight? To answer these questions, David Hubel and Torsten Wiesel used
cats as their model. The two researchers first sewed shut one eye of a kitten
and left it shut for three months. After the three-month period, the sutures
were removed and the retina signaling to the visual cortex (the signal
receiving center in the brain) from both eyes was evaluated. They did the
same for adult cats as well. In the case of kittens, the eye that had been sewed
shut for three months had an abnormally low signal response by the visual
cortex, whereas the untreated eye had an abnormally high response. For
adult cats, no differences were found between the treated and untreated eyes.

Through these experiments, Hubel and Wiesel identified two important aspects of visual development. First, there is a critical period shortly after birth where the connections between the retina and the brain seem to be cemented. Knowing this, surgeons now perform surgery as soon as safely possible in cases of congenital cataracts, which has greatly improved outcomes. Second, when there is a visual impairment (or loss of sight) in one eye, the remaining functioning eye can compensate and redistribute nerves to the brain. This compensation provides an opportunity for scientists to study ways to bypass damaged brain signals and develop alternate ways to better see the world. For these and other discoveries in their laboratory, Hubel and Wiesel shared the 1981 Nobel Prize in Physiology or Medicine.

§

Cats have also been important elements in famous literature, being a favorite topic of Nobel Prize winners. When Doris Lessing was announced as the 2007 Nobel Prize in Literature, the Swedish Academy described her as "that epicist of the female experience, who with scepticism, fire and visionary power has subjected a divided civilisation to scrutiny." Her books often included topics that were hard to face: colonialism, feminism, violence, social norms. Lessing, however, had a softer side that came through in books she wrote about her fondness for cats. Her real and literary cats all had names, some plain (Grey Cat), some fanciful (Rufus the Survivor), some regal (El Magnifico).

§

One of the longest running musicals shares both a topic and name: *Cats*. The musical has been seen by over 70 million people worldwide and has grossed billions of dollars. Andrew Lloyd Webber, whom most people have heard of, has been credited with the musical. *Cats* would have never existed, however, without a set of poems written by Thomas Stearns Eliot (pen name, T. S. Eliot), winner of the 1948 Nobel Prize in Literature. Like Doris Lessing, T. S. Eliot had a serious side to his writing. He and Lessing also shared a fascination with cats that began in childhood. Cats were never far from his mind. Beginning in the 1930s, Eliot began writing poems to his godchildren. He later compiled the poems into a book titled *Old Possum's Book of Practical Cats*. The "possum" in the title was based on an actual nickname that was once given to Eliot. The cats in the poems were given whimsical names such as Rum Tum Tigger, Jellylorum, Bombalurina, Mungojerrie, Mister Mistoffelees, and Old Deuteronomy. Andrew Lloyd Webber borrowed these same names for *Cats*. But Webber did more than that. By setting T. S. Eliot's poems to music, he allowed these poems to be enjoyed in a new way. Clearly, pussycats and Nobel Prizes can be a winning combination.

Dogs

In December 1921, fourteen-year-old Leonard Thompson lay in a Toronto hospital bed. He was nearly six feet tall but weighed only sixty-five pounds. Diabetes had caused his organs to fail. His hair was falling out. Remarkably, four months later, a healthy – although still diabetic – Thompson left the hospital, saved because of the discovery of insulin. And Dog 33.

Frederick Banting and Charles Best at the University of Toronto were working with dogs that had had their pancreases removed. It was known that the pancreas was the organ that secreted a substance that helped regulate blood sugar levels. Without a functioning pancreas, the dogs became diabetic. Banting and Best wanted to treat these dogs with an extract from newborn cow pancreas, which contained high amounts of a compound they termed "isletin". Many dogs had the surgery performed, and many quickly died. One dog, however, did survive. Her name was Marjorie. On December 7, 1921, Banting and Best injected Marjorie with a purified extract of isletin (later renamed insulin). The dog's blood sugar levels dropped and could be controlled by injecting insulin.

Marjorie. Courtesy of Thomas Fisher Rare Book Library, University of Toronto.

Because of the success with Marjorie, permission was given for Leonard Thompson to be experimentally treated with an injection of Banting's purified isletin. The young man's blood sugar levels dropped immediately. After tweaking the timing and dosage of insulin, his blood sugar levels were regularly controlled. After regaining his strength, Thompson was released from the hospital. In their May 1922 scientific paper in *The Journal of Laboratory and Clinical Medicine*, Banting (who received the Nobel Prize in Physiology or Medicine the next year) and Best included two photos of Marjorie, identifying her simply as Dog 33.

Leonard Thompson lived another thirteen years before succumbing to pneumonia. He was buried alongside his parents and sister. The headstone has an inscription at the bottom that has meaning for both Leonard and Marjorie: *Ever Remembered.*

§

Dogs have also been important elements in the works of winners of the Nobel Prize in Literature. John Steinbeck used dogs as allegories in several of his books. Typically, these dogs were symbols of impending hardship, dependency, or the value of humans. In *The Grapes of Wrath*, a family dog dies beside a roadside garage after being struck by a car. The dog's death becomes an omen for what lies ahead for the family. In *Tortilla Flat*, a bulldog with a vicious reputation approaches a man but decides not to bite his leg after sensing goodness in the man. In *Cannery Row*, a grizzled old man gives a puppy to a group of young ruffians, who realize that the dog is now dependent on them to survive. *Of Mice and Men* includes both a puppy and an old dog. The puppy is accidentally killed by its owner. The old dog is put down. Both deaths symbolized the weak being ruled by the strong.

In real life, John Steinbeck loved having dogs as companions, although he would have been forgiven if he had disciplined his English Setter puppy, Toby, who apparently took a dislike towards *Of Mice and Men*. Left alone one night – a mistake that no puppy owner should make – Toby ate half of the manuscript. Or as Steinbeck described it, made confetti out of it. Maybe Toby was correct. The final version of the novel was met with critical acclaim, being adapted to the first of four film versions just two years later.

Of course, here the story takes a new twist. When the book was first published in 1937, the price was $2.00. Today, a first edition, first printing hardcopy with dust cover can be yours for a mere $4,500. But that is still a deal compared to the $13,000 that was paid at auction in October 2023 for a 2 × 2–inch fragment from the original 1936 draft that Toby gnawed on.

The fragment, which came from the Mary Steinbeck Dekker Collection, mentions both main characters, Lennie and George. The piece might have gone for much more if it had Toby's pawprint to support its authenticity.

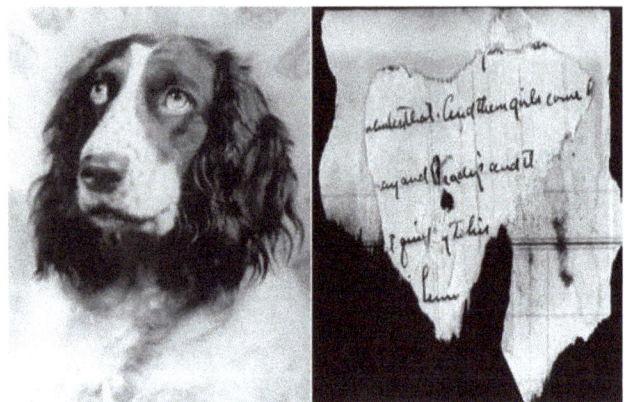

Toby the English Setter and a remaining manuscript fragment from Steinbeck's *Of Mice and Men* after Toby finished his chewing. Courtesy of the Martha Heasley Cox Center for Steinbeck Studies, San Jose State University.

§

Last, there is Foxtrot, the only animal to lay claim to a Nobel Prize. Foxtrot is a true rags-to-riches story. Born in Bangladesh and separated from his mother, four-week-old Foxtrot latched onto the staff of the United Nations World Food Programme (WFP) and has been with the WFP ever since.

Gemma Snowdon and Foxtrot (wearing his official ID badge). Courtesy of the World Food Programme.

The WFP is a major relief group that provides food assistance and other vital services to people affected by war, natural disasters, and pandemics. As the WFP's goodwill ambassador, Foxtrot – who sometimes wears a super-dog cape – can be found working alongside his human companions, his role being to maintain morale. Foxtrot is also an identifiable face of the WFP that helps with fundraising. He even has his own Instagram account administered by his typist and assistant, Gemma Snowdon, a WFP communications officer.

In 2020, the WFP was honored with the Nobel Peace Prize. As an official member of the team who even had his own ID badge, there were no ifs and buts about it. A dog had won the Nobel Prize. When the announcement came, Foxtrot typed (or maybe dictated) on his Instagram account, "Wowee." A true doggone achievement!

CHAPTER SEVEN

All Work and No Play

There is a seventeenth-century proverb that, if updated, would read, "All work and no play make Jack and Jill dull people." According to its author, James Howell, working constantly without taking a break to enjoy life makes a person boring. If that is the case, one might think that Nobel laureates must be as dull as it gets.

How wrong that would be. If you carried on a conversation with a Nobel laureate, you would likely learn that they have worked hard at their craft but have not let work consume their life. They have not been chained 24/7 to a typewriter, laboratory bench, chalkboard, or negotiating table. Peeling off the outside layers, you would find someone who has outside interests and hobbies. Even hobbies that contributed to a Nobel Prize.

Accordion	French horn	Pinochle
Amateur radio	Gardening	Railway tables
Antique collecting	Golf	Raising chickens
Art collecting	Graphic design	Raising snakes
Artist (e.g., painter)	Greek dancing	Robotics
Astronomy	Guitar	Rock climbing
Baking bread	Harmonica	Rollerblading
Banjo	Harmonium	Rugby
Barbershop quartet	Hiking	Running/marathons
Baseball	Hockey	Safecracking
Bass	Hockey stick collecting	Saxophone
Bass guitar	Horse riding	Scrabble
Bassoon	Hunting	Sculpting
Beekeeping	Huqin	Seashells
Bird watching	Ice dancing	Skiing
Bodybuilding	Ice skating	Skydiving
Bongo drums	Insect collecting	Snooker
Bonsai	Jewelry	Soccer/football
Bowling	Jigsaw puzzles	Softball
Boxing	Jiu-Jitsu	Squash
Bridge	Judo	Stained glass
Butterfly collecting	Juggling	Stamp collecting
Cacti	Karate	Stonemason
Calligraphy	Kayaking	Sudoku

Camping	Limericks	Swimming
Cello	Kite surfing	Table tennis
Checkers	Magic	Tambourine
Chess	Mandolin	Target shooting
Choir	Mayan hieroglyphics	Tennis
Christmas	Meteorology	Trombone
Cigars	Miniature dollhouses	Trumpet
Civil War	Model airplanes	Tuva throat singing
Clarinet	Model trains	Ukulele
Coin collecting	Motorcycle collecting	Viola
Cooking	Mountain climbing	Violin
Croquet	Music composition	Volleyball
Crossword puzzles	Oboe	Washboard
Cycling	Opera	Water polo
Fencing	Organ	Wines/winemaking
Flute	Photography	Woodworking
Flyfishing	Piano	Yodeling
Fossil collecting	Postcard collecting	Zither

Accordions to Zithers, Classical to Rock

Nobel laureates have played many musical instruments, from the accordion to the zither, enough to create an orchestra with a full string section, wind instruments, percussionists, keyboards, and more. Of course, not everyone's tastes lean towards a full orchestra. Not to worry. There is enough musical talent among Nobel laureates to pull together a string quartet or a wind ensemble. Even a bluegrass or jazz band. Wyomingite, mandolin player, and 2007 Nobel Peace Prize winner Jason Shogren is the front man for the band J Shogren Shanghai'd, whose style is what he calls Wyoming Mountain Blues. If you are especially lucky, you may be invited to perform a set with harmonica player Jim Allison and his blues band, The Checkpoints. This 2018 Nobel laureate may even introduce you to his friend Willie Nelson.

If rock 'n' roll is your thing, there are Nobel laureates to keep you grooving to the music. Two recipients of the 2022 Nobel Prize in Chemistry, Carolyn Bertozzi and Morten Meldal, play guitar and have a rock 'n' roll past. Bertozzi, who plays both bass guitar and keyboards, has more famous roots. She once played the keyboard in a band named Bored of Education with Tom Morello, the guitarist who later created the band Rage Against the Machine. Rhythm guitarist Meldal is resurrecting his old band, Carlsband. Meldal loves playing reggae music, which makes him a loner among his bandmates. His passion for the guitar is reflected in his hobbies of collecting as well as building guitars.

Carolyn Bertozzi with a bass guitar she keeps in her laboratory. Courtesy of Christopher Michel.

Morten Meldal with one of his self-built guitars. Courtesy of Björn Gunér/Sveriges Radio.

§

No singer, instrumentalist, or composer has ever won a Nobel Prize for their music. Astute Minnesotans might think otherwise, since Hibbing-born singer-songwriter Bob Dylan won a Nobel Prize in 2016. But his prize was not for music, it was for literature. His choice as the prize winner that year was met with both outrage and praise. The millions who listen closely to his many Billboard Top 100 hit songs know that Dylan is proof that lyrics contain words, and sung words can evoke emotion as much as the printed words.

§

It turns out that Bob Dylan is not the first Nobel laureate to have composed a Billboard #1 hit. That honor goes to Charles Dawes, the 1925 Nobel Peace Prize recipient, who also was Calvin Coolidge's vice president. Prior to his time in Washington, Dawes lived in Chicago, where, in his spare time, he would compose songs on his piano. In 1911, he wrote a piece called "Melody in A Major," which he shared with a friend. Unbeknownst to Dawes, his song made the rounds. Dawes only became aware of his tune's popularity when he strolled by a music store and saw a large poster of himself in the window along with a copy of the sheet music. Several years later, RCA Victor produced the first 78 rpm record containing the song. In 1951, lyricist Carl Sigman added words to "Melody in A Major," changing the name to "It's All in the Game." Singer Tommy Edwards's version was a chart-topping hit for six weeks in 1958. Even Bob Dylan has shown a liking for "It's All in the Game," singing it at many of his concerts. Perhaps it's the only time a Nobel laureate has covered the song of another Nobel laureate!

Amateur Radio to Yodeling

Outside of music, Nobel laureates have spent their time participating in at least a hundred other hobbies. They tinker with electronics, play card games, solve puzzles, relax in the garden, camp, hunt, fish, and bake bread. In some cases their choices of hobbies, or how they found them, have been – to put it mildly – surprising.

Take, for example, boxing. With a participation rate of one to two percent of the population, boxing is not unusual. But to have boxers among Nobel Peace Prize winners does seem unusual. Of the three boxing laureates, two won the Peace Prize and one was a peace activist.

Nelson Mandela, antiapartheid activist, 1993 Nobel Peace Prize winner, and the first president of South Africa, was an amateur boxer as a young man. In 1956, Mandela was one of the 156 South Africans arrested and prosecuted as part of the infamous Treason Trial. After sitting in the dock all day, he would spar on the roof of Jerry Moloi's boxing gym. Although acquitted, Mandela later spent twenty-seven years in prison for political reasons. He performed a daily boxing routine in prison. In his autobiography, *Long Walk to Freedom*, Mandela wrote, "Boxing is egalitarian. In the ring, rank, age, colour and wealth are irrelevant."

Nelson Mandela sparring with coach and mentor
Jerry Moloi, 1957. Drum Social
Histories/BAHA/ Africa Media Online.

The twenty-sixth president of the United States, Theodore "Teddy" Roosevelt, had the ability to bring warring countries to the discussion table. But the 1906 Peace Prize winner was also a pugilist. Roosevelt took up boxing at Harvard during the days when it was a bare-knuckle sport. He continued to box for many years afterward, even while he was in the White House. Roosevelt ordered that his staff find him sparring partners, even a professional boxer if one was available. In 1905, a miliary aide, Captain Dan Moore, who also happened to be a cousin of Roosevelt's wife Edith, was recruited for a sparring session. Moore punched the president so hard that it detached his retina, causing a loss of sight in his left eye. After that episode,

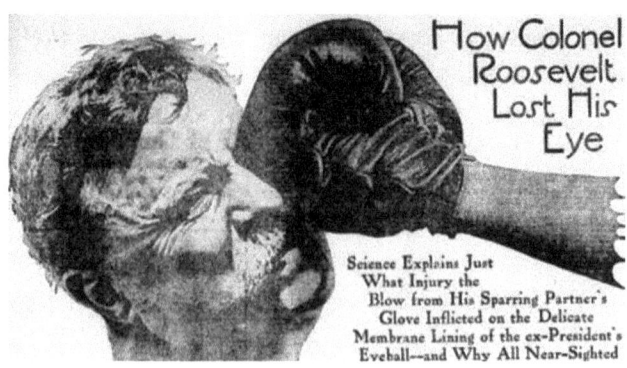

Article published in 1917 after the press learned about Teddy
Roosevelt's lost eyesight. Courtesy of *Richmond Times Dispatch*.

Roosevelt switched to a safer sport: jiu-jitsu. Interestingly, Roosevelt was able to hide his injury from the public for the next twelve years before the press finally got wind of it.

The third Nobel laureate who laced up the gloves also boxed above his level of expertise. In the mid-1990s, World Boxing Association champion Ray "Boom Boom" Mancini was in his dentist's office when the dentist noted that he had another patient who was a boxing fan and who would like to meet Mancini. The patient's name was Bob Dylan. After an invitation to meet at a private gym, Mancini walked in to see Dylan in a corner lacing up boxing gloves. Dylan motioned for Mancini to climb into the ring and the sparring began. Dylan assured Mancini that he could take a punch, so Mancini used his jab to tag Dylan several times. After the second round, Dylan walked over to Mancini and said, "Ray, could you lay off those headshots? I still have a few songs left in there."

§

Compared to boxing, chess is a more reserved game. Chess playing by Nobel laureates goes all the way back to Emil Von Behring and the first Nobel Prizes in 1901. Theodore Roosevelt was an avid chess player. As with his boxing prowess, he self-proclaimed extreme confidence when it came to chess. During a European trip as a child, Roosevelt saw the expert chess playing machine named "Ajeeb the Wonderful" – a mechanical humanoid-

Ajeeb the Wonderful. TCS 1.183, Harvard
Theatre Collection, Harvard University,
public domain.

looking device. When Ajeeb later made its way to America, one of the people lining up to challenge Ajeeb was said to be Roosevelt. The machine won. This was not surprising, since Ajeeb was controlled by a master chess player behind the machine.

§

Can cigar collecting be a hobby? British prime minister Winston Churchill, winner of the 1953 Nobel Prize in Literature, smoked up to ten cigars a day and had between three and four thousand cigars stored in a room near his study. The cigars were even categorized for easier selection. One could argue whether this was a collection or an over-the-top habit. It is nearly impossible to find a photograph of the British Bulldog without a cigar. During a trip to the United States in 1931, Churchill forgot that he was not in England, where they drive on the left side of the road. He was struck by a car and hospitalized. When he returned to England a few weeks later, he was transferred by ambulance to his flat for recuperation. The press photograph documenting his return home showed Churchill on a stretcher – smoking a cigar. A year later, Churchill was hospitalized again, this time for paratyphoid. No surprise that the press photographs of Churchill leaving a nursing home on the ambulance stretcher showed him puffing away.

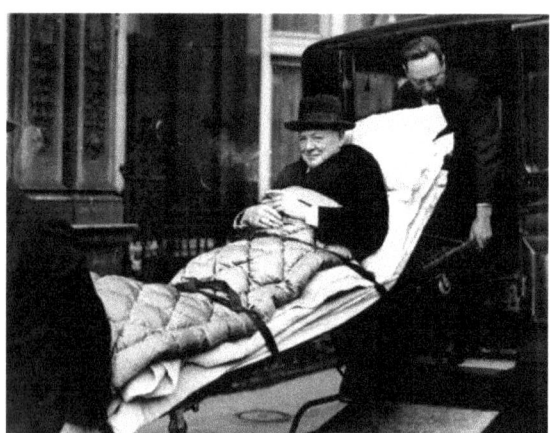

Not even in the ambulance yet and Churchill had to have his cigar. Album/SuperStock/Sydney Morning Herald.

While prime minister during World War II, Churchill needed to go on high altitude flights that required him to be fitted with an oxygen mask. It has been claimed that Churchill had a customized oxygen mask created with a hole in it so he could smoke his cigars while in flight. Ever the savvy politician, Winston Churchill also used cigars as a tool for controlling a negotiation table. He would stick a thin wire down the front half of his cigar so that the ashes would not fall off but instead would grow to a point that their length distracted those with whom he was negotiating. Churchill went through as much scotch as he did cigars. But scotch drinking is a separate hobby, so we will leave it there.

§

In the same way that Winston Churchill was rarely seen without a cigar, laureate Jeffrey Hall, who was mentioned earlier, has rarely been seen without a civil war hat on his head. In fact, Hall wore one of his many Civil War officer's hats in his official Nobel Prize photo. His fascination with the Civil War, especially the Union Army, started some forty years ago during a family vacation to Gettysburg, Pennsylvania. Listening to his father describe the loss of life on this battlefield, Hall realized how easily the North could have lost the war. Hall has become somewhat of an expert on the Civil War, even teaching classes at Brandeis University. Quite a change from studying fruit flies. If you are a fan of military history, then you have something common with a Nobel laureate.

§

Ice dancing became an Olympic sport in 1976. It is like ballroom dancing, except that it involves ice skaters who perform waltzes and other pattern dances. Not a common way to spend one's spare time. So, how did the 2003 laureate in economics, Robert F. Engle III, become a champion ice dancer?

Robert Engle and partner Amy Engeler at a competition in Obertsdorf Germany. Courtesy of Robert Engle and Amy Engeler.

The answer becomes clearer once you know that it all started with the hope for romance. As a graduate student, he began dating a girl who was an ice skater. She asked him to go to a local figure skating club to learn to ice dance. Engle soon recognized that there was a shortage of men who ice danced. Even more incentive to show up. And the girlfriend? She left both the club and Engle.

§

Physicists are known for helping to unlock the secrets of the universe. But one physicist was known for unlocking safes. Richard Feynman, quantum physicist and 1965 Nobel Prize winner, was in his spare time a proficient safecracker. In the 1940s, Feynman, who contributed to the development of the atomic bomb, was stationed at a secret and restricted facility near Los Alamos, New Mexico. Given the isolated location and the need to avoid drawing any attention to the facility, there was no entertainment or active social life. To keep himself amused, Feynman played around with the locks on the filing cabinets. It wasn't long before he had that figured out.

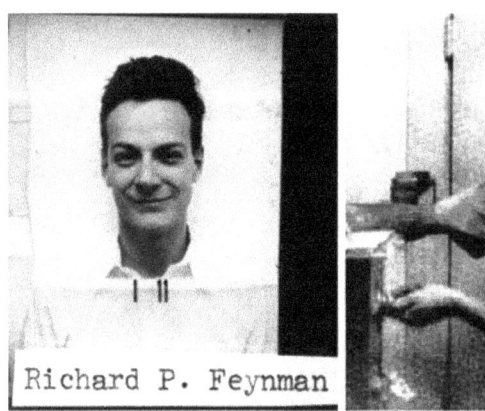

Left, Richard Feynman's Alamos ID. Right, Feynman opening a safe. Left, Wikimedia Commons, public domain; right, School of Math and History, St. Andrews University, Scotland.

He graduated to safes as his next targets and soon cracked the secrets to their combinations. Feynman once visited a secure uranium facility and, by opening selected safes, showed how security needed improvement. After he left, the colonel in charge ordered staff to change the combination to their safes if Richard Feynman was in their office, near their office, or even walked through their office.

§

Eduard Buchner, the 1907 laureate in chemistry, liked to climb mountains in his native home of Germany. Not exactly unusual. What was unusual was his yodeling. When the sun rose, Buchner's yodeling began. When the sun set, his yodeling continued. Buchner yodeled from mountaintops. He yodeled from balconies, often late into the night. On the eve of his wedding, Buchner celebrated by yodeling his way through town. He nearly spent the rest of the night in the drunk tank.

Hobbies Contributing to Nobel Prizes

Barbara McClintock, winner of the 1983 Nobel Prize in Physiology or Medicine, played banjo in a jazz band when she was younger. She liked jazz because, as a musical style, it included both structure and variation at the same time. There was a background melody that served as a tune's foundation. But there was room for improvisation, where one musician could change patterns and add a new, unexpected element to the music. McClintock never became a professional musician, choosing science – specifically genetics – as a career. McClintock studied maize (corn). Not the uniform yellow corn seen in grocery stores, but the multicolored ornamental corn used to decorate porches and fences in the fall.

When McClintock began her career, scientists believed that the genes in corn kernels (every individual kernel on an ear of corn is a unique organism) were organized like a string of pearls, where information was genetically transferred as a whole string. Mutations in the order of the pearls could occur, which resulted in offspring with a malformation or defect (negative impact). But McClintock noted something unusual. The kernel color patterns were too random, changed too often between subsequent generations, and were not deleterious to the corn. Thus, these were not mutations passed on to a future generation but instead something that occurred within an individual kernel (kind of like cut and paste of the pearl sections responsible for color formation).

She called these gene sections "jumping genes" because they behaved just like musical notes jumping around in a jazz piece. Among the overall expected order of the genes (the background melody), a small switch of location introduced a new variation (an improvisation) in another gene. Had Barbara McClintock not realized that genetic patterns paralleled jazz patterns, it might have been decades before the emergence of modern gene editing therapies.

§

Baseball has been the favorite sport of numerous Nobel laureates. Max Thieler (1951 Nobel Prize in Physiology or Medicine) loved the Brooklyn Dodgers. Laureate Adam Riess majored in physics but wrote his college research paper on baseball's 1919 Black Sox Scandal. Economist and 2002 Nobel laureate Ben Bernanke is a huge Washington Nationals fan. Bernanke

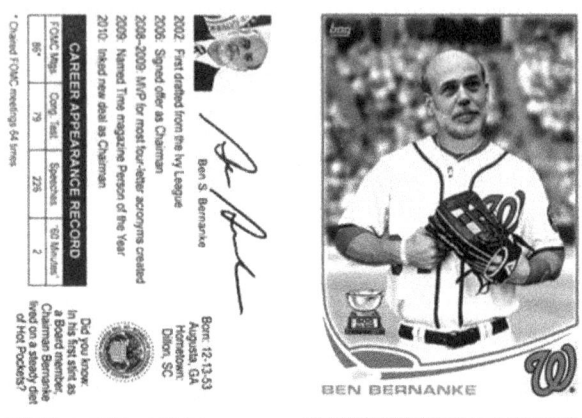

Ben Bernanke's unofficial Washington National baseball card.
Federal Reserve, public domain. PD-USGov-Federal Reserve.

even has his own custom baseball card – a replica of a Nationals player's card created by the staff when Bernanke stepped down as chair of the Federal Reserve.

No one, however, has taken a love for baseball all the way to a Nobel Prize like Yuan Lee. Since the age of eight, Yuan Lee was crazy about baseball. While his parents believed their son was in the library studying, Yuan was in the local park gripping a wooden pole as a bat. When baseball became a recognized sport in Taiwan, Yuan, then eleven years old, dreamed of playing on a real baseball team. His parents agreed that he could join a team – not knowing that he had secretly been playing ball for several years – if his grades held up. Fortunately, Yuan Lee was smart and passed all his exams without a lot of studying. Lee's grades remained good enough that he was admitted to college and later won the 1986 Nobel Prize in Chemistry for his work on cross-molecular beams studies, where beams of atoms were aimed in a crossing motion and the angular scattering of particles was measured after the beams collided. Yuan Lee admitted that the project would not have come to mind if he had not remained fascinated by another type of particle collision he encountered in school. Not in mathematics or physics class. The collision phenomenon that had inspired Yuan Lee's prize-winning research was a foul ball deflecting off a bat.

§

Alexis Carrel, winner of the 1912 Nobel Prize in Physiology or Medicine, was a young French surgeon when France's president was killed in 1894 by an assassin who plunged a dagger deep into the politician's chest. The surgeons attempting to save the French leader were only familiar with crude suturing techniques where blood vessels were simply pushed together and a suture was wrapped around them (think wrapping a Band-Aid around a finger). Their patient died. Carrel felt in his heart that physicians could do better and vowed to find ways to improve surgical outcomes. His solution? Take up embroidery.

He started by going to local sewing supply stores and purchasing fine lace needles and silk thread that did not kink and slid easily through material. But identifying the best needles and threads only went so far. Carrel sought out Marie Anne Leroudier, the finest embroideress in France. Leroudier was renowned for her gold thread techniques used on the curtains in the Paris Opera House. She met with Carrel in the evenings at her house, where he learned how to make thread go precisely where it was intended, how to work one handed, and delicately pierce only partly through the fabric.

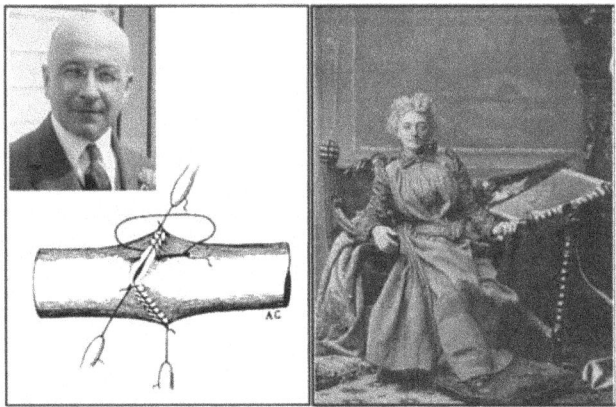

Left, Alexis Carrell and his anastomosis technique based on sewing lessons from Marie Anne Leroudier. Left, Lyon Medical, 1902, public domain; right, Inconnu, cliché du Tout-Lyon, Wikimedia Commons.

Carrel purportedly became so proficient that he could squeeze five hundred stitches into a cigarette paper. Ever improving his skills, Carrel eventually developed a triangulation technique that was inspired from his embroidery lessons, in which three sutures were used as anchor points to protect a blood vessel during surgery. Today we refer to it as end-to-end anastomosis. In honor of the woman who taught the young surgeon, perhaps a more fitting name would be the Leroudier-Carrel technique.

§

How did a physics professor contribute to a Nobel Peace Prize? Through his skydiving hobby, of course. Steven Singletary, a professor at the University of North Carolina Pembroke, had been an avid skydiver for close to twenty-five years. He was also a skydiving instructor and a recognized parachute rigger. This experience made him an expert in parachute design and aerodynamics, which came to the attention of the United Nations World Food Programme (WFP).

A well-equipped Steven Singletary hanging out of a plane. Courtesy of Steven Singletary.

The WFP had been fighting hunger in places such as South Sudan, but progress was poor. The organization had tried trucking food into famine-stricken areas, but the food was hijacked by warlords. The next plan was to use airdrops from planes. Food could be dropped safely. The containers of gasoline and oil needed for cooking, however, would explode on even minor impact. Seeking a better parachute, the WFP reached out to a consultant who told them that the man they needed was a former colleague, Steven Singletary. Singletary helped the WFP develop parachute prototypes. Improving on his designs, Singletary and the WFP ultimately created a parachute that could be successfully used to provide lifesaving sustenance to African nations. The WFP, with Steven Singletary as part of the team, won the 2020 Nobel Peace Prize.

First drop test of a Singletary parachute prototype, 2016. Courtesy of Steven Singletary.

§

And then there is golf, which author John Feinstein described as "a good walk spoiled." For many individuals, this is decidedly true. But for Satoshi Omura, his walks on the golf course led to the 2015 Nobel Prize in Physiology or Medicine. Omura, a biochemist, spent much of his career investigating potential pharmaceutical agents produced from natural origins, primarily by microorganisms in soil. What better way to use his time than to combine his career and his hobby.

Left: A low-handicap golfer, Satoshi Omura, playing the St. Andrews Old Course, the ancient Home of Golf, in Scotland. Right: The pocket collection kit Omura carries everywhere. Photographs by and courtesy of Andy Crump.

Omura carried (and still carries) a plastic bag during his rounds of golf to collect soil samples for future evaluation. In a wooded area at the edge of the golf course at the Kawana Hotel (where Marylin Monroe and Joe DiMaggio honeymooned), he took a tiny bag of soil from which a unique microbe was isolated that produced a chemical subsequently refined into the drug ivermectin, which kills many internal and external parasites that plague people and animals around the globe.

So, the next time your significant other asks where you are going with those golf clubs, tell them that you are going out to help save the world from pestilence and disease.

CHAPTER EIGHT

Don't Try This at Home

As part of a study of submarine safety, the British scientist J.B.S. Haldane placed himself in a decompression chamber to study the effects of gases and pressures on the body. He ended up perforating his eardrums. Haldane found the one bright spot to damaging one's eardrums, reporting, "The drum generally heals up; and if a hole remains in it, although one is somewhat deaf, one can blow tobacco smoke out of the ear in question, which is a social accomplishment."

Haldane also exposed himself to high levels of carbon monoxide, which gave him debilitating headaches. Another experiment testing the effects of high oxygen treatment resulted in a seizure and several crushed vertebrae. Haldane never received the Nobel Prize, but it was for reasons that had nothing to do with his proclivity towards self-experimentation. In fact, self-experimentation and unauthorized experimentation have occurred in science with surprising frequency, in some cases resulting in discoveries that directly contributed to a Nobel Prize.

Pierre Curie

In 1898, future Nobel laureate Pierre Curie, along with his wife Marie and Henri Becquerel, discovered a new element they named radium. The trio observed that this element could destroy tumor-type cells faster than healthy cells. To demonstrate radium's potential in curing cancer, while lecturing to

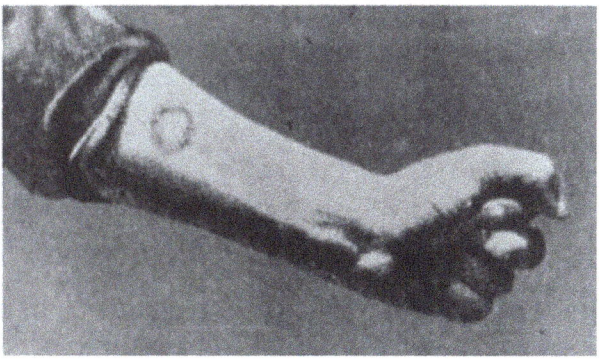

Pierre Curie's arm showing scar from radium burn. Academie des Sciences Institut de France.

a group of scientists, Pierre Curie rolled up his sleeve and showed a burn on his arm caused by the self-application of radium salts. Unfortunately, the highly radioactive and toxic nature of radium was unrealized at the time. Despite vigorous washing, Curie's arm likely remained radioactive for years. Had he not been killed in an accident in 1906, Curie might have later died from cancer, the same disease he sought to cure with radium.

Werner Forssmann

If there was an Easier to Ask for Forgiveness than Permission Club, Werner Forssmann would have been a charter member. As a freshly minted physician, Forssmann knew that the accurate diagnosis and treatment of cardiac disease was limited by an inability to see what was really going on in a patient's heart. He proposed to his new chief that passing a catheter into the arm and threading it into the heart might be the solution. His chief disagreed. Undeterred, Forssmann convinced a nurse, Gerda Ditzen, to supply him with a long piece of urinary catheter tubing. Ditzen, providing consent to be the test subject, allowed Forssmann to strap her to an operating table. But after restraining her, Forssmann proceeded to cut his own arm and passed the catheter through his veins and into his heart. He then released Ditzen and asked her to help him walk to the X-ray department, where they proceeded to collect an image of the catheter successfully lying in his right atrium.

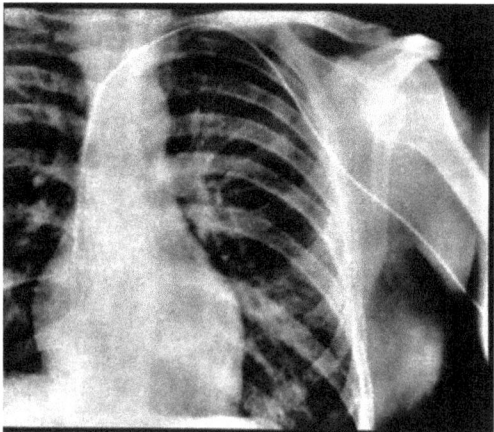

Werner Forssmann's cardiac catheterization on himself. Note the white catheter leading from his arm to his heart. Werner Forssmann, 1929, Wikimedia Commons, public domain. PD-US.

His self-experimentation was considered so outrageous that he was ostracized as a surgeon and finally ended up in a urology practice. Fortunately, two physicians at Columbia University and Bellevue Hospital, André Frédéric Cournand and Dickinson Richards, continued to improve the technique to the point that cardiac catheterization gradually became accepted as a valuable tool in patient care. This ultimately led to Cournand, Richards and Forssmann being awarded the 1956 Nobel Prize in Physiology or Medicine "for their discoveries concerning heart catheterization and pathological changes in the circulatory system."

Donald Glaser

Donald Glaser won the 1960 Nobel Prize in Physics for his invention of the bubble chamber, which allowed for detection of subatomic particles. The bubble chamber consisted of a sealed glass bulb about the size of a thumb, filled with liquid (often volatile ethyl ether). Glaser first submerged the glass bulbs in cold oil and then transferred the bulbs into extremely hot oil, superheating the liquid into a high energy state. Not exactly the routine experiment one would want to perform at home or alone in a laboratory.

In an article in *The Guardian* (March 5, 2013) covering Glaser's death, writer Frank Close described the concept of the bubble chamber:

> Glaser was a 25-year-old faculty member at the University of Michigan when he conceived of the bubble chamber. A homely example of the effect that Glaser developed is that of opening a bottle of beer. Releasing the bottle's cap causes a sudden drop in pressure, whereby bubbles start to rise through the liquid. Glaser's idea was to keep a liquid at high pressure, near to its boiling point. In such circumstances, a gentle drop in pressure will cause the liquid to start boiling, an effect well known to mountaineers who, at altitude, can brew a cup of tea at lower temperatures than at sea level.

This was a great description for multiple reasons. First, it clearly described the bubble chamber concept in a way that is easily understood. Second, given the title of this book, it illustrated another relationship between beer and the Nobel Prize. And third, this future Nobel laureate once used beer in an unauthorized experiment that nearly got him thrown out of the University of Michigan.

During the development of the bubble chamber, Glaser had performed calculations that led him away from the use of water as the liquid because it had too high of a surface tension and critical pressure. But to be sure that his prediction was correct, he decided to test a fluid that he knew created bubbles: beer. Glaser brought a case of beer into the laboratory around two a.m. He chilled a bottle of beer and pulled the cap off. Not surprisingly, the beer foamed a little, but that was all. Taking the experiment a step further, he followed the complete protocol by cooling the beer, followed by quickly transferring the bottle into a hot oil bath and releasing the pressure. There was bubbling alright. In fact, the experiment was a little too successful.

Donald Glaser with bubble chamber, 1956.
Bentley Historical Library, University of
Michigan Digital Collections. CC BY 4.0.

Hot beer went all over, including hitting the ceiling. The laboratory now smelled like a brewery. If that wasn't bad enough, the university had a policy that alcohol could not be brought anywhere near campus buildings. To make matters even worse, the chairman of Glaser's department was a strict teetotaler. Luckily, Glaser was forgiven and kept his job. In my opinion, he should have at least been suspended for wasting perfectly good beer.

Barry Marshall

Parents have often lamented that their children were giving them ulcers. We can thank Barry Marshall and Robin Warren for vindicating children around the world. Marshall had read about pathologist Warren's findings that gastric biopsies from patients with chronic gastritis had bacteria growing on the surface. Looking for a research project, he contacted Warren and the two began a collaboration.

They hypothesized that a bacterium, *Helicobacter pylori*, was the cause of chronic gastritis and gastric ulcers in patients, and that treatment with antibiotics could eradicate the bacterium and heal the ulcer. Many professionals in the field disagreed. Marshall and Warren's hypothesis went against the belief that stress, spicy foods, and other lifestyle factors were the source of patients' problems.

The only way to prove their theory was to show cause, effect, and cure on a healthy subject who would provide informed consent to the experiment. According to Barry Marshall in a 2006 interview in *New Scientist*, "I was the only person informed enough to consent, so I decided to be my own guinea pig." But first, he needed to be sure he was free of the *Heliobacter*. Marshall asked his department head to perform an endoscopy on him. His boss agreed, only after adding that he was going to ask no questions and wanted no answers. Marshall was negative for the bacteria, which provided the go-ahead for his next move.

Barry Marshall drinking his swarming brew brimming with a billion bacteria.
Barry Marshall, kind approval for reproduction of images.

Telling no one, including his wife, Marshall then drank a concentrated broth of the bacteria. Several days later, nausea and vomiting set in, along with horrible breath and an unhappy wife. A biopsy demonstrated severe gastritis and tissue inflammation. A course of antibiotics eliminated the symptoms. Marshall had shown cause, effect, and cure. Barry Marshall and Robin Warren were awarded the 2005 Nobel Prize in Physiology or Medicine "for their discovery of the bacterium *Helicobacter pylori* and its role in gastritis and peptic ulcer disease.

EPILOGUE

You and the Nobel Prize

Well, you have made it to the end of this book. If I have succeeded, you have learned two things about the Nobel Prizes and the individuals who have won the prizes. First, the Nobel Prizes are not so distant or abstract that they have little to do with our everyday lives. Who would have thought that items we regularly encounter – a refrigerator, pigeon, sticky tape, or chair – have some link to a Nobel Prize or a Nobel laureate.

Second, Nobel laureates have accomplished things that we only dream about, yet in many ways they are no different from the rest of us. They have the same hobbies. They like rock 'n' roll, country, jazz, and reggae music. They do surprisingly dumb things like giving oneself an ulcer to prove a point. They play with ants. They are pacifists and pugilists in one individual.

In 2024, the Nobel Prize Museum began displaying a selection of items from its collection of artefacts donated by laureates. These objects were important to these individuals' lives and achievements, ranging from the mundane to the imaginative. One of these you have already read about: Nelly Sachs's suitcase in which she carried everything she owned as she escaped Nazi Germany. Other items included an undamaged dress found in the rubble of a burned-out village years after a Nobel Peace Prize winner escaped from soldiers who raided a wedding. The dress was a symbol of survival and good rising from the ashes. Another was a jug of Tide detergent. There was an accordion, a set of keys, a typewriter, coloring book, belt, photocopy machine, jigsaw puzzle, slide rule, bicycle, and dozens more items. Individually and collectively a sort of Nobel time capsule. They were not just objects, they were peoples' stories.

Take the origin of this book. A cold beer in a college guest house was the genesis of an idea that became *Beer and the Nobel Prize*. In fact, I think a beer bottle would be the perfect addition – the artefact – to my time capsule. That way, if someone asks "What's with the beer bottle?" I can answer "Well, there's a story behind that."

My challenge to you is to identify artefacts that have influenced your life. I bet you will find that your artefacts are just as meaningful as those of famous people. To you they might be just objects, yet they might be stories waiting to rise to the surface. And it is stories that keep life interesting.

Acknowledgments

When I began writing *Beer and the Nobel Prize*, I wanted to include images that would help bring the stories to life for the reader. Among the book's many images are rare photos, newspaper clippings, family photos, archive materials, sculptures, artefacts, and previously unpublished professional photographs. The captions beneath the images credit the sources, but it is important to acknowledge how helpful these academic institutions, libraries, museums, artists, companies, photographers, and more were when I sought permission to include an image in the book.

I also wanted to stay true to the stories while being fair to the people and places in the book. In some cases, I wanted to verify a detail such as a date, location, conversation, or surrounding circumstance by contacting relatives and colleagues as well as the laureates themselves. Without fail, these individuals not only responded but provided added insight into the story I was trying to tell or an interesting fact to include. To these individuals I remain grateful.

Like people, books go through maturation phases that require guidance from others. Authors need to know when they are straying away from the right path or need assurance that they are still on the right path. Authors require advice from people who can be both advocates and critical readers, sometimes at the same time. I was fortunate to have colleagues who excelled at both. Lauren Talalay, Steve Bank, Karis Crawford, and Kenneth Vinton went beyond catching typos. Together with my copyeditor extraordinaire Skye Loyd, they provided me with helpful suggestions for improving the flow (and sometimes clarity) of what I was trying to write. *Beer and the Nobel Prize* is a better book because of them.

Bibliography

PREFACE

Steve Hartman, "Everybody has a story, flashbacks," CBS News, January 11, 2010. https://www.cbsnews.com/news/everybody-has-a-story-flashbacks/.

NOBEL PRIZE WORD ASSOCIATION

Chair

"Guests share seats with laureates at Nobel Museum," Sveriges Radio, December 6, 2015.

Seashells

Allison Marsh, "The long road to today's cochlear implant," *IEEE Spectrum*, January 8, 2022.

Riley Montgomery and Gauri Mankekar, "From silence to sound: Graeme Clark's cochlear implant," *Cureus* 16, no. 9 (2024): e68580.

Water

Elisabeth Davenas et al., "Human basophil degranulation triggered by very dilute antiserum against IgE," *Nature* 333, no. 6176 (1988): 816–818.

Declan Butler, "Nobel laureates face libel suits from 'water memory' researcher," *Nature* 389, no. 6650 (1997): 427.

Luc Montagnier et al, "Electromagnetic signals are produced by aqueous nanostructures derived from bacterial DNA sequences," *Interdisciplinary Science* 81, no. 2 (2009): 81–90.

Martin Enserink, "Nobelist escapes 'intellectual terror' to pursue ideas in China," *Science* 330, no. 6012 (2010): 1732.

Robin Weiss et al., "Luc Montagnier (1932–2022)," *Science* 375, no. 6586 (2022): 1235.

Refrigerator

Matthew Trainer, "Albert Einstein's patents," *World Patent Information* 28, no. 2 (2006): 159–165.

"Einstein's 'Automatic Concrete-Volks-Refrigerator,'" Carl von Ossietzky University, http://www.presse.uni-oldenburg.de/f-aktuell/05-363.html.

Gene Dannen, "The Einstein-Szilard refrigerators," *Scientific American* (January 1, 1997): 90–95.

Ross Pomeroy, "Albert Einstein's forgotten inventions," Real Clear Science, Feb 8, 2018.

Yogurt

Philip Mackowiak, "Recycling Metchnikoff: Probiotics, the intestinal microbiome and the quest for long life," *Frontiers in Public Health* 1 (2013): 52.

"Ilya Metchnikoff," Alimentarium.org. https://www.alimentarium.org/en/story/ilya-metchnikoff.

Scott Podolsky, "Metchnikoff and the microbiome," *The Lancet* 380, no. 9856 (2012): 1810–1811.

Luba Vikhanski, "The man who blamed aging on his intestines," *Nautilus*, May 12, 2016.

"A walk through Danone's history," Medium, November 21, 2016.

Coin

Daniel Kahneman and Amos Tversky, "Prospect theory: An analysis of decision under risk," *Econometrica* 47, no. 2 (1979): 263–292.

"Loss Aversion," HireMinds, March 23, 2019.

"Daniel Kahneman," The Nobel Prize, https://www.nobelprize.org/prizes/economic-sciences/2002/kahneman/facts/.

Toothpaste

"Development of Fluoride Toothpaste," IU Historical Marker – 2020, https://honorsandawards.iu.edu/awards/honoree/10568.html.

"Alfred Curie and tho-radia," Museum of Radiation, Sept. 5, 2020.

"A success story … from near extinction to top selling brand," Old Time Radio Researchers, https://www.otrr.org/FILES/Articles/Danny_Goodwin_Articles/Pedsodent.htm.

"Who is the irium girl?" Oscar Rennebohm Library at Edgewood College, November 18, 2021.

Pajamas

Simon Frantz, "Six tips for surviving the Nobel prize festivities in Stockholm," *The Guardian*, December 8, 2011.

Annica Haglund, "Golden-haired women awaken Nobel laureates on Lucia day," *AP News*, December 12, 1990.

THE PHONE CALL

You Can't Tell Anyone

Richard Henderson

"Richard Henderson, Nobel Prize in Chemistry 2017: Official interview," The Nobel Prize, December 2017, https://www.nobelprize.org/prizes/chemistry/2017/henderson/interview/.

Barry Marshall

"Barry Marshall: Nobel Prize Conversations," The Nobel Prize, https://www.nobelprize.org/prizes/medicine/2005/marshall/podcast/.

Barry Marshall and Adrienne Marshall, "Fish and chips and a Nobel Prize: Remembering Robin Warren," *Medical Journal of Australia Insight*, September 9, 2024.

Flying High

Richard Ernst

Angela Herring, "The making of a scientist," *Northeastern Global News*, April 7, 2014.

Edvin Moser

"'Why are you calling me?' May-Britt Moser's reaction to the Nobel Prize call," posted by The Nobel Prize, YouTube, https://www.youtube.com/watch?v=bY_9gjEECOo.

Milton Friedman

"The Nobel Prize in Economics, 1976," *Milton Friedman at the Income Distribution Conference sponsored by the Hoover Institution*, January 29, 1977. https://digitalcollections.hoover.org/objects/57491.

Relatives and Neighbors
Joshua Angrist
Adam Reinherz, "Sarah and Stan Angrist on how to raise a Nobel Prize winner," *Pittsburgh Jewish Times*, October 15, 2021.

"Telephone interview with Joshua Angrist," posted by The Nobel Prize, YouTube, https://www.youtube.com/watch?v=Bh_CXgAdou8.

Ardem Patapoutian
"Ardem Patapoutian interview," The Nobel Prize, February 2022, https://www.nobelprize.org/prizes/medicine/2021/patapoutian/interview/.

Paul Milgrom
"Interview with Paul Milgrom," The Nobel Prize, March 2021, https://www.nobelprize.org/prizes/economic-sciences/2020/milgrom/168950-milgrom-interview-march-2021/.

Sorry, Wrong Number
Norman Ramsey
"Norman F. Ramsey, Nobel Prize in Physics 1989: When the Nobel call went astray," posted by The Nobel Prize, YouTube, https://www.youtube.com/watch?v=215ImAEd3rU.

Donald Cram
"Carpet cleaner mistaken for Nobel Prize winner – The Tonight Show with Johnny Carson – 1988," YouTube, https://www.youtube.com/watch?v=tNoJL6LGtqY.

Stephen Braun, "Nobel for rug cleaner? It's a prize foul-up," *Los Angeles Times*, October 15, 1987.

Don't Ruin My Walk
Brian Stallard, "Barbara McClintock: Free to discover," Cold Spring Harbor Laboratory, March 23, 2020.

You can't fool me
May-Britt Moser
"'Why are you calling me?' May-Britt Moser's reaction to the Nobel Prize call," posted by The Nobel Prize, YouTube, https://www.youtube.com/watch?v=bY_9gjEECOo.

Benjamin List and David MacMillan
"Benjamin List and David MacMillan, Nobel Prize laureates in chemistry 2021, settle a bet," posted by The Nobel Prize, YouTube, https://www.youtube.com/watch?v=2z1MCrdFKdM.

"Interview with David MacMillan," February 2022, The Nobel Prize, https://www.nobelprize.org/prizes/chemistry/2021/macmillan/183036-david-macmillan-interview-february-2022/.

David MacMillan, personal communications.

I'm a Schnook
Martin Chalfie
"The Nobel Prize call," The Nobel Prize, https://www.nobelprize.org/prizes/themes/the-nobel-call/.

BEYOND THE GRAVE

The Obituary

"The woman behind the Nobel peace prize," Nobel Peace Center, November 27, 2019.

Evan Andrews, "Did a premature obituary inspire the Nobel Prize?" History.com, July 23, 2020.

Colin Schultz, "Blame sloppy journalism for the Nobel Prizes," *Smithsonian Magazine*, October 9, 2013.

Who's Buried in Alfred Hollis's Grave?

Louise Foxcroft, "Grave historical doubts," *The Guardian*, September 8, 2000.

"Who's really buried beneath this headstone?" *Irish Times*, October 11, 2000.

Lara Marlowe, "WB Yeats: Papers confirm bones sent to Sligo were not poet's," *Irish Times*, July 18, 2015.

Only Strong Pallbearers Need Apply

Martin Peretz, "Body of evidence," *The New Republic*, February 14, 2005.

Joel Lubenau and Jean-Luc Pasquier, "The radioactive remains of Pierre and Marie Curie," *The Invisible Light* 37 (2013): 12–26.

Miriam Hyman, "The half-life of Marie Curie, *Lyceum*, December 14, 2019.

The Nomadic Life of Einstein's Brain

Michael Paterniti, "Driving Mr. Albert," *Harper's Magazine*, October 1997.

William Kremer, "The strange afterlife of Einstein's brain," BBC World Service, April 18, 2015.

Matt Blitz, "How Einstein's brain ended up at the Mütter Museum in Philadelphia," *Smithsonian Magazine*, April 17, 2015.

Buried, Exhumed, Reburied, Exhumed, Reburied . . .

Marvine Howe, "Leftists mourn Neruda at rites," *New York Times*, September 26, 1973.

Stephen Phelan, "Exhuming Neruda," *Boston Review*, May 22, 2013.

Adam Feinstein, "Poet Pablo Neruda to be reburied in Chile following judge's ruling," *The Guardian*, February 23, 2015.

"Chile reburies remains of Nobel prize-winning poet Pablo Neruda," BBC News, April 26, 2016.

Colin Dwyer, "Pablo Neruda didn't die of cancer, experts say. So what killed the poet?" National Public Radio, October 23, 2017.

Karma

Elad Zeret, "The Yiddish Don Juan," Ynetnews.com, January 7, 2015.

Elisabeth Bumiller, "Errata and incongruities at Isaac Bashevis Singer's grave," *New York Times*, June 19,1997.

Jonathan Mark, "The last Isaac Bashevis Singer story," Jewish Telegraphic Agency, December 4, 1997.

"Last Singer tale finally gets proper ending years after writer's death, typo on gravestone is fixed," *Baltimore Sun*, June 19, 1997.

LUCK AND THE NOBEL PRIZE

The Lucky Discovery of Insulin

Louis Rosenfeld, "Insulin discovery and controversy," *Clinical Chemistry* 48, no. 12 (2002): 2270-2288.

James Wright, "Almost famous: E. Clark Noble, the common thread in the discovery of insulin and vinblastine," *Canadian Medical Association Journal* 167, no. 12 (2002): 1391-1396.

James Brody, "Insulin was discovered 100 years ago – but it took a lot more than one scientific breakthrough to get a diabetes treatment to patients," *The Conversation*, July 21, 2021.

Lars Ryden and Jan Lindsten, "The history of the Nobel prize for the discovery of insulin," *Diabetes Research and Clinical Practice* 175, no. 5 (2021): 108819.

Lucky Encounters

Michael Rosbash and Jeffrey Hall

Lawrence Goodman, "How Rosbash and Hall did it," Brandeis Now, October 2, 2107.

Karen Given, "The pickup basketball game that led to a Nobel Prize," WBUR News, March 16, 2018.

Katalin Karikó and Drew Weissman

Ting Yu, "How scientists Drew Weissman (MED'87, GRS'87) and Katalin Karikó developed the revolutionary mRNA technology inside COVID vaccines," *Bostonia*, November 18, 2021.

"Honoring mRNA pioneers Katalin Karikó and Drew Weissman," Northwell Health Insights, September 9, 2022.

Harry Markowitz and Eugene Fama

Stephen Foerster, "How four Nobel laureates got lucky," Medium, October 17, 2022.

Eugene Fama, "A brief history of finance and my life at Chicago," *Chicago Booth Review*, April 7, 2014.

Nelly Sachs and Selma Lagerlof

"Literature laureate Nelly Sachs' suitcase donated to the Nobel Prize Museum," Nobel Prize Museum, April 26, 2023.

Tereixa Constenla, "A noble act. The female writer who fought Nazis and machismo," El Pais, December 26, 2017.

Stephanie Newman, "Sweden's gate: On the life and literature of Selma Lagerlöf & Nelly Sachs," Majuscule, October 22, 2020.

Kirsten Krick-Aigner, "Nelly Leonie Sachs," Jewish Women's Archives, October 24, 2023.

Alfred Nobel and Bertha von Suttner

Ingvill Bryn Rambøl, "The woman behind the Nobel Peace Prize," Nobel Peace Center, November 27, 2109.

Reverend Sally Bryan, "Bertha Von Suttner," Iowa State University, May 16, 1994.

Thomas Annesley, "The pen (pal) is mightier than the sword," *Clinical Chemistry* 67, no. 6 (2021): 917–918.

Lucky Experiments

Karl Landsteiner

Karl Landsteiner, "On agglutination of normal human blood," *Wiener Klinische Wochenschrift* 14 (1901): 1132–1134.

Probability Calculator. Calculator.net, https://www.calculator.net/probability-calculator.html.

Jakub Marian, "Blood type distribution by country in Europe,"
https://jakubmarian.com/blood-type-distribution-by-country-in-europe/.

Otto Stern

Bretislav Friedrich and Dudley Herschbach, "Stern and Gerlach: How a bad cigar helped reorient atomic physics," *Physics Today* 56, no. 12 (2002): 53–59.

Samik Dutta, "A century of spin!" Medium, December 11, 2023.

Zack Savitsky, "The (often) overlooked experiment that revealed the quantum world," *Quanta Magazine*, December 5, 2023.

Andrew Geim

Andre Geim, "Random walk to graphene," The Nobel Prize, December 8, 2010.

Sarah Lewis, "The deliberate amateur," Slate, May 21, 2014.

Arturo Robertazzi, "Curiosity, ingenuity, persistence – Andre Geim's random walk to the discovery of graphene," From Atoms to Words, October 20, 2023.

WAYWARD MEDALS

Opening Paragraph

Pierre-Henry Deshayes, "1,001 ways to lose a Nobel Prize," Phys.org, September 28, 2018.

I Think You Have My Medal

"A unique gold medal," The Nobel Prize, March 11, 1998.

Burglars and Bunglers

Kay Miller medal

Pat Reavy, "Arrest leads to the recovery of a Nobel prize," *Deseret News*, January 13, 2007.

Ernst Lawrence medal

Janet Gilmore, "Nobel Prize medal stolen from Lawrence Hall of Science is found, student arrested," *UC Berkeley News*, March 7, 2007.

"UC Berkeley student pleads no contest to Nobel Prize theft," TheUnion.com, October 3, 2007.

Rabindranath Tagore medal

"8 detained for Tagore medal theft," *The Tribune online edition*, March 27, 2004.

Roy Glauber medal

Bob Sprague, "Arlington police track down suspect nabbed in Nobel theft," Arlington.com, April 16, 2010. http://philosophyofscienceportal.blogspot.com/2010/04/non-noble-nobel-theif-caught.html.

Laurel Sweet, "Cops: Nobel-napper helped self to Harvard prof's Arlington digs," *Boston Herald*, April 16, 2010.

Ernest Hemingway medal

Dan Sheehan., "Back in 1986, the Castros helped retrieve Hemingway's stolen Nobel Prize," *LITHUB*, March 15, 2021.

So Why Were You in Fargo?

Roshina Jowaheer, Nobel Prize winner questioned by airport security over award," Yahoo News, October 12, 2014.

Going Once, Going Twice, Sold!

Aristide Brand medal

Pierre-Henry Deshayes, "1,001 ways to lose a Nobel Prize.," Phys.org, September 28, 2018.

"How much for that Nobel Prize in the window?" Phys.org, October 3, 2015.

Dmitry Muratov medal

Lidia Kelly, "Russian journalist's Nobel Peace Prize fetches record $103.5 million at auction to aid Ukraine children," Reuters.com, June 11, 2022.

James Watson medal

Brendan Borrell, "Watson's Nobel medal sells for US$4.1 million," *Nature*, December 4, 2014.

Ian Sample, "Billionaire bought James Watson's Nobel Prize medal in order to return it," *The Guardian*, December 9, 2014.

Leon Lederman medal

Sarah Kliff, "A Nobel Prize-winning physicist sold his medal for $765,000 to pay medical bills," Vox, October 4, 2018.

Carlos Saavedra Lamas medal

Associated Press, "1936 Nobel Peace Prize won by Argentinian prime minister to be auctioned in Baltimore," *New York Post*, March 13, 2014.

Sam Creighton, "The price of peace? Nobel Prize, awarded to Argentina's foreign minister in 1936 is bought for $1.16 million after being discovered in South American pawn shop," *The Daily Mail*, March 27, 2014.

Hidden in Plain Sight

"A unique gold medal," The Nobel Prize, March 11, 1998.

Robert Krulwich, "Dissolve my Nobel Prize! Fast! (A true story)," National Public Radio, October 3, 2011.

Savannah Gignac, "The invisible prize," American Institute of Physics, 2023.

A MEDAL FOR MICKEY MOUSE

Mice

Lindsay Dodgson, "2 YouTube pranksters successfully nominated a British reality star for the Nobel Peace Prize to prove how meaningless Trump's nominations are," *Business Insider Nederland*, October 1, 2017.

Insects

Mosquitos

Francis Cox, "History of the discovery of the malaria parasites and their vectors," *Parasites & Vectors* 3 (2010): 5.

Kumaravel Rajakumar and Martin Weisse, "The centennial year of Ronald Ross' epic discovery of malaria transmission: An essay and tribute," *Pediatric Research* 43, Suppl 4 (1998): 155.

Lice

Ludwik Gross, "How Charles Nicolle of the Pasteur Institute discovered that epidemic typhus is transmitted by lice: Reminiscences from my years at the Pasteur Institute in Paris," *Proceedings of the National Academy of Sciences USA* 93, no. 20 (1996): 10539–10540.

"Charles Nicolle. Nobel lecture: Investigations on typhus," The Nobel Prize,
  https://www.nobelprize.org/prizes/medicine/1928/nicolle/lecture/.

Ants

"Feynman's Ants," Mathpages.com,
  https://www.mathpages.com/home/kmath320/kmath320.htm.

Fruit flies

Ilona Miko, "Thomas Hunt Morgan and sex linkage," *Nature Education* 1, no. 1 (2008):
  143.

Alfred Sturtevant, "Thomas Hunt Morgan," *National Academy of Sciences* (1959), 283–
  325.

Jacob Hamblin, "'A dispassionate and objective effort': Negotiating the first study on the
  biological effects of atomic radiation," *Journal of the History of Biology* 40, no. 1
  (2007): 147–177.

Rebecca Barr, "Milestone 13 (1980): How the fruit fly gets its stripes," *Nature Reviews
  Neuroscience*, July 1, 2004.

Richard Axel, "Scents and sensibility: A molecular logic of olfactory perception," The
  Nobel Prize, December 8, 2004,
  https://www.nobelprize.org/prizes/medicine/2004/axel/lecture/.

Ewen Callaway and Heidi Ledford, "Medicine Nobel awarded for work on circadian
  clocks," *Nature* 550, no. 7674 (2017): 18.

Aleksandra Nall et al., "Caffeine promotes wakefulness via dopamine signaling in
  Drosophila," *Scientific Reports* 6 (2016): 20938.

Saleh Adnan et al, "Caffeine as a promotor of sexual development in sterile Queensland
  fruit fly males," *Science Reports* 10 (2020): 14743.

Butterflies

"Gabriel Garcia Marquez's yellow butterflies," April 27, 1024.
  http://josephscissorhands.blogspot.com/2014/04/gabriel-garcia-marquezs-yellow.html.

Lizbeth Diaz, "Fans pay tribute to Nobel laureate Garcia Marquez in Mexico City,"
  Reuters, April 21, 2014.

Camille Parmesan, "Detection of range shifts: General methodological issues and case
  studies of butterflies," in G.R. Walther, C.A. Burga, and P.J. Edwards (eds.),
  "Fingerprints" of climate change (Boston: Springer, 2001).

Sarah Bloodworth, "The butterfly effect," Texas Parks and Wildlife, July 2019.

Bees

Lars Chittka, "Dances as windows into insect perception," *PLoS Biology* 2, no. 7 (2004):
  898–900.

Tina Heidborn, "Dancing with bees," Max Planck Research,
  https://www.mpg.de/789351/W006_Culture-Society_074-080.pdf.

Tania Munz, *The dancing bees: Karl von Frisch and the discovery of the honeybee
  language* (University of Chicago Press, 2016).

Housefly

Robert Krulwich, "There's a fly in my urinal," National Public Radio, December 19, 2009.

Blake Evans-Pritchard, "Aiming to reduce cleaning costs," *Works That Work*, Winter 2013.

Christopher Ingraham, "What's a urinal fly, and what does it have to with winning a Nobel
  Prize?" *Washington Post*, October 9, 2017.

Birds

Chickens

Peyton Rous, A transmissible avian neoplasm, sarcoma of the common fowl. *Journal of
  Experimental Medicine* 12, no. 5 (1910): 1696–1705.

Katherine Irving, "Transmissible tumors, 1909," The Scientist, January 3, 2023.

Matthew Tontonoz, "How a chicken helped solve the mystery of cancer," Memorial Sloan Kettering Cancer Center, December 27, 2017.

Susan Okie, "U.S. scientists win Nobel Prize," *Washington Post*, October 10, 1989.

Kiona Smith, "Meet the Dutch army doctor who discovered vitamin B and cured a deadly disease," Forbes, August 13, 2018.

Christiaan Eijkman, "Antineuritic vitamin and beriberi," The Nobel Prize, https://www.nobelprize.org/prizes/medicine/1929/eijkman/lecture/.

Geese

Saul McLeod, "Konrad Lorenz: Theory of imprinting in psychology," Simply Psychology, June 16, 2023.

Eckhard Hess, "Imprinting in animals," *Scientific American* 198 (1958): 81–93.

Tania Munz, "'My Goose Child Martina': The multiple uses of geese in the writings of Konrad Lorenz," *Historical Studies in the Natural Sciences* 41, no. 4 (2011): 405–446.

Pigeons

Sindy Harris, "Pigeons show up for National Pigeon Appreciation Day," *Jacksonville Review*, June 19, 2023.

Brian Wilson and Jonathan Schisler, "Sir Hans Adolf Krebs: Architect of metabolic cycles. *Laboratory Medicine* 41, no. 3 (2010): 377–380.

Geoff Brumfiel, "Big bang's ripples: Two scientists recall their big discovery," National Public Radio, May 20, 2014.

Claudia Dreifus, "How two pigeons helped scientists confirm the big bang theory," *Smithsonian Magazine*, February 19, 2014.

Ali Sundermier, "The strongest evidence of the big bang was almost mistaken for pigeon droppings," *Business Insider*, October 12, 2016.

"June 1963: Discovery of the cosmic microwave background," American Physical Society, https://www.aps.org/archives/publications/apsnews/200207/history.cfm.

Cats

Eating cat food

Leff Guo, "This Kardashian headline shows why two Nobel winners say the economy is broken," *Washington Post*, October 29, 2015.

Jason Zweig, "'Phishing for Phools': A Q&A with George Akerlof and Robert Shiller," *Wall Street Journal*, September 15, 2015.

Schrödinger's Cat

Melody Kramer, "The Physics Behind Schrödinger's Cat Paradox," *National Geographic*, August 14, 2013.

Joshua Rapp Learn, "Schrödinger's cat experiment and the conundrum that rules modern physics," *Discover Magazine*, May 11, 2021.

Hubel and Wiesel

David Hubel and Torsten Wiesel, "Effects of monocular deprivation in kittens," *Naunyn-Schmiedeberg's Archives of Pharmacology*, 248, no. 6 (1964): 492–497.

Dina Lienhard, "David H. Hubel and Torsten N. Wiesel's research on optical development in kittens," *Embryo Project Encyclopedia*, October 11, 2017.

Doris Lessing

Ellen Vrana, "Doris Lessing on our inimitable human companions and how to cross that which separates us," The Examined Life, https://theexaminedlife.org/library/on-cats.

T. S. Eliot

Pronoy Sarkar, "When T. S. Eliot wrote poems about cats," Off the Shelf, September 5, 2014.

"80th Anniversary of Old Possum's Book of Practical Cats," T. S. Eliot Prize. October 5, 2019.

Dogs
Marjorie
Matthew Klingle, "The multiple lives of Marjorie: The dogs of Toronto and the co-discovery of insulin," *Environment His*tory 23, no. 2 (2018): 368–382.
Toby
Katie Yee, "Fun fact: John Steinbeck's dog ate the first draft of *Of Mice and Men*," Literary Hub, May 27, 2020.
"Fragment of *Of Mice and Men* original manuscript sold for $13,000, Steinbeck's sword for $3,500," Fine Books & Collections, October 30, 2023.
Foxtrot
Jason Beaubien, "Lost pup finds new life as humanitarian mascot in refugee camp," National Public Radio, April 22, 2019.
Tanmay Sahay, "Meet Foxtrot, an Instagram puppy that has become a mascot for Bangladesh's Rohingya refugees," Scroll.in, February 20, 2020.
Jason Beaubien, "Nobel Peace Prize goes to the dog (aka the mascot of WFP)," National Public Radio, October 9, 2020.

ALL WORK AND NO PLAY
Accordions to Zithers, Classical to Rock
Jason Shogren and Jim Allison
Steve Kiggins, "Jason Shogren," *University of Wyoming Focus Magazine*, https://www.uwyo.edu/business/focus/pdfs/focus-winter-13.pdf.
Rachel Humphrey, "When your harmonica player wins the Nobel Prize," *The Cancer Letter* 44, no. 37 (October 5, 2018).
Joe Palca. "Cancer scientist jams with Willie Nelson one more time," National Public Radio, June 9, 2016.
Carolyn Bertozzi and Morten Meldal
Manuel Ansede. "Carolyn Bertozzi, Nobel laureate in chemistry: 'We've invented a miniature lawn mower for cancer cells,'" *El Pais*, January 21, 2023.
Sam Scott, "Life is sweet," *Stanford Magazine*, March 2022.
Oliver Bodh Larsen, "Nobel Prize winner Morten Meldal: 'I can assure you that it is not always the best projects that are funded,'" Uniavisen, May 15, 2023.
Bob Dylan
"The Nobel Prize in Literature 2016," The Nobel Prize, https://www.nobelprize.org/prizes/literature/2016/summary/.
Catherine Dent, "How did Bob Dylan win the Nobel Prize in Literature?" The Collector, September 30, 2023.
Charles Dawes
Bill Kaufmann. The Melodious Veep. American Enterprise Institute, January 1, 2004.
Ron Grossman. Charles Dawes was a banker, general, vice president – and hit songwriter. *Chicago Tribune*, January 12, 2025.

Amateur Radio to Yodeling
Boxing
"Remembering Mandela, the boxer," Grantland, December 6, 2013.

"Mandela: A legacy that reaches the whole world," World Boxing Association, June 18, 2020.

Sudiksha Kochi, "Fact check: Theodore Roosevelt's eyesight was permanently damaged by military aide during boxing match," *USA Today*, November 6, 2021.

"Teddy Roosevelt's little-known secret," *Chicago Tribune*, Oct. 7, 2002.

Gordon Marino, "Ray 'Boom Boom' Mancini on his surreal time sparring with Bob Dylan in the boxing ring," *The Daily Beast*, May 24, 2021.

Chess

John Thorn, "Ajeeb, the Eden Musée chessman," Gotham History, May 11, 2015.

Cigars

Truett Smith, "Winston Churchill: A cigar smoking tribute," Smoking Pipes, November 28, 2018.

David Savona, "Smoking and drinking like Churchill," Cigar Aficionado, May/June 2018.

Richard Carleton, "Hacker: Out of the ashes," Robb Report.

Nikola Budanovic, "Winston Churchill was such a passionate smoker, he asked that his oxygen mask for high altitude flights be customized to fit a cigar," War History Online, November 27, 2017.

Civil War hats

Catherine Meyers, "A Nobel Laureate's historical hats," Inside Science, October 2, 2017.

Regina Nuzzo, "Profile of Jeffrey C. Hall," *Proceedings of the National Academy of Sciences USA* 102, no. 46 (2005): 16547–16549.

Ice dancing

"Robert F. Engle III – Biographical," The Nobel Prize, https://www.nobelprize.org/prizes/economic-sciences/2003/engle/biographical/.

Safecracking

Richard Feynman, *Surely you're joking, Mr. Feynman!* (New York: W.W. Norton & Company, 1985), 137–155.

Yodeling

Lothar Jaenicke, "Centenary of the award of a Nobel Prize to Eduard Buchner, the father of biochemistry in a test tube and thus of experimental molecular bioscience," *Angewandte Chemie International Edition* 46, no. 36 (2007): 6776–6782.

Hobbies Contributing to Nobel Prizes

Jazz

"Episode 5: Barbara McClintock, Nobel Prize winner and jazz banjoist," The Jazzy Chemist, YouTube, https://www.youtube.com/watch?v=4bkCC9v3lCs.

Patrick Parr, "Barbara McClintock (1902–1992): Fighting the male establishment," *The Humanist*, March 21, 2016.

"Music meets science," Tumble, https://www.sciencepodcastforkids.com/single-post/music-meets-science.

Baseball

Patrick Gillespie. "Ben Bernanke: 6 fun facts you didn't know," CNN, October 6, 2015.

Binyamin Appelbaum, "A parting gift as Ben Bernanke hangs up his cleats," *New York Times*, January 31, 2014.

"Paul Harvey – Yuan T. Lee," posted by Harold Cheetham, YouTube, https://www.youtube.com/watch?app=desktop&v=TibOrlzq9Sw.

"Baseball inspired work that led to Nobel chemistry prize," United Press International, October 16, 1986.

Embroidery
Paul Craddock, "The 19th century French embroiderer who made modern organ transplant possible," *The Daily Beast*, May 23, 2022.

Robert Cusimano et al., "The genius of Alexis Carrel," *Canadian Medical Association Journal* 131, no. 9 (1984): 1142–1150.

Paul Craddock, "Three early transplant pioneers," The History Reader, https://www.thehistoryreader.com/historical-figures/three-early-transplant-pioneers/.

Skydiving
Tomeka Sinclair, "UNCP educator uses skydiving and classroom knowledge to help starving people," *The Robesonian*, October 30, 2020.

"UNCP physics professor contributes to United Nation's Nobel Peace Prize," University of North Carolina Pembroke, November 20, 2020.

Golf
Aldric Hama, "Amazing science: The soil sample from an Izu golf course that changed the world," Japan Forward, January 8, 2022.

DON'T TRY THIS AT HOME
J.B.S. Haldane
Eleanor Harris, "Eight scientists who became their own guinea pigs," *New Scientist*, Mach 11, 2009.

Pierre Curie
Richard Mould, "The discovery of radium in 1898 by Maria Sklodowska-Curie (1867–1934) and Pierre Curie (1859–1906) with commentary on their life and times," *British Journal of Radiology* 71, no. 852 (1998): 1229–1254.

Eleanor Harris, "Eight scientists who became their own guinea pigs," *New Scientist*, March 11, 2009.

Werner Forssmann
Mark Nicholls, "Werner Forssmann Nobel Prize for physiology or medicine 1956: Mark Nicholls looks at the courageous role Werner Forssmann played in the development of cardiac catheterization and the subsequent award of the 1956 Nobel Prize for his endeavours," *European Heart Journal* 41, no. 9 (2020): 980–982.

Ian Kerridge, "Altruism or reckless curiosity? A brief history of self experimentation in medicine," *Internal Medicine Journal* 33, no. 4 (2003): 203–207.

Donald Glaser
Frank Close, "Donald Glaser obituary," *The Guardian*, March 5, 2013.

Rupert Cole, "The art of boiling beer," Science Museum, July 29, 2013.

Barry Marshall
Alison George, "Hard to Swallow," *The New Scientist*, December 6, 2006.

Barry Marshall and Meghan Azad, "Q&A: Barry Marshall: A bold experiment," *Nature* 514, no. 7522 (2014): S6–7.

www.ingramcontent.com/pod-product-compliance
Lightning Source LLC
Chambersburg PA
CBHW051535120626
46551CB00012B/1241